THE PATIENT ENGLISH
SIMON HENRY

Copyright © 2001
Illustrations © 2001 WPC

Editors: Luke Chaput de Saintonge and S.J. Harris

First published in Great Britain
by Nightingale Press, an imprint of
Wimbledon Publishing Co. Ltd
London P.O. Box 9779 SW19 7ZG

ISBN: 1903222 24 9

Produced in Great Britain
Printed and bound in Hungary

All rights reserved. No part of this publication may be reproduced, transmitted or stored in a retrieval system in any form or by any means without permission in writing from Nightingale Press.

SIMON HENRY'S

THE PATIENT ENGLISH

An Unconventional Guide to a Conventional People

ILLUSTRATED BY MARK BENNINGTON

Nightingale Press
an imprint of Wimbledon Publishing Company
LONDON

ABOUT THE AUTHOR

Simon Henry was born in 1970 in Yorkshire, England and was educated at University College London and Brasenose College, Oxford.

He has worked as a journalist, book reviewer and columnist for a variety of British and US newspapers and magazines. He is also the author of Nightingale's controversial publication, *A Tourist's Guide to the British*.

He now works as a full-time on-line journalist, writing national and international news stories.

He lives in his native Yorkshire.

CONTENTS

1.	*Introduction*	page 6
2.	*The Royal Family*	page 11
3.	*Social Class*	page 24
4.	*The Pub*	page 43
5.	*The Weather*	page 60
6.	*The Queue*	page 72
7.	*English Dialects*	page 86
8.	*Food*	page 101
9.	*Transport*	page 113
10.	*Sport*	page 130
11.	*Culture (the Arts)*	page 147
12.	*Oxford: an English University*	page 162
13.	*Politics*	page 171
14.	*England and the Outside World*	page 183
15.	*Conclusion*	page 189

One Introduction

One: INTRODUCTION

Come in then and wipe your feet on your way

This is a book about England, for a world which speaks its language but misunderstands its people. Here, at last, the mysterious conventions of this strange nation are explained for all. For the first-time visitor planning a trip to England, at least a cursory understanding of this land of cream tea, cream crackers, cream flannel trousers and grey clouds is vital. The visitor ignores the advice of *The Patient English* at his peril. For the patient English themselves, it provides an insight into their own absurd, eccentric and plainly ludicrous customs. It is the author's hope that it may even raise a half-smile of recognition among his long-suffering fellow countrymen.

Now that most of the factories and mines have been closed down, England's main source of wealth is its tourism industry. It is perhaps a bit risky, then, for us to embark on this candid journey. Nevertheless, the author feels duty-bound to lay bare the truths behind the glossy leaflets of the English Tourist Board - and hang the consequences, be they rioting on the streets of Paris, trade sanctions from Washington, or someone mumbling, "oh ... mmm" in London.

Careful reading of the following chapters will equip the visitor to deal with the potential embarrassment, bewilderment, and humiliation which threaten the tourist in England.

Most visitors spend their time in a state of complete confusion because they misunderstand the intricate set of rules governing the lives of the English. As a result, countless newcomers have committed rudimentary social gaffes, leading to 'scenes' - an English euphemism for any moments of skin-crawling social humiliation. The English live in constant fear of such moments and avoidance of them is as much in their interests as it is the visitor's.

England has attracted foreigners from the start of its history. The Romans invaded, but left bored and damp. The Vikings came from Scandinavia for the temperate climate, but left damp and smelling of wet fur. The Normans popped over for a quick invasion, and stayed: being French, they were already rather moist.

Having invaded, the invaders naturally became the most important people in the land. Seeing as the peasants were too stringy to eat, the newcomers took their land instead and forced the natives to become their servants. Thus the aristocracy was born. To this day, they still refuse to eat the poor, God bless their ever bountiful generosity.

In time, the peasantry metamorphosed into the working class (with industrialisation) and later the underclass (with de-industrialisation). The aristocracy has retained its exalted social position to this day. However, wealth has become more evenly spread over the centuries as a thriving middle class has evolved. It is this enormous section of society that provides England with much of its famed mediocrity, conservatism ...and patience.

Non-invading foreigners have always been welcome on England's shores, but any further inland and they were sent down holes to dig. These became the working class. In more recent times, Commonwealth citizens from India, Pakistan and the West Indies, who were invited to replace a workforce decimated in WWII, brought with them curries and spicy foods. This started a love of foreign cuisine which has seen the country released from the prison of over-cooked vegetables and suet. Chicken tikka masala has now replaced the roast dinner as the nation's favourite dish.

Irish and Commonwealth immigrants struggled patiently to be accepted by a sceptical native population, and now provide an integral ingredient in the national culture. However, the casual visitor doesn't have decades of experience and assimilation to help him blend in. Never mind, for this book is every bit the substitute for having lived thirty years as a third generation immigrant. No, really, it is.

Previous visitors complained they were not advised to bring an umbrella and a sheepskin coat for their two week August vacation. They wish they had been told to sit on the left hand side of the road in the ubiquitous English traffic jam. They wish they had been informed that Scotland was not in England. Many unseemly incidents might have been avoided had this book been published earlier. The author notes his apologies to those who have only just been able to buy it, and his lack of sympathy to those who refuse to invest. Be it on your own heads.

Meanwhile the English may benefit from a few home truths. Why, we ask, do they still believe themselves to be the world's best sportsmen when their teams are ritually humiliated by others who have only just learnt the rules the English themselves invented? How can they retain a Royal Family whose only apparent contribution is to keep the tabloid press in business? Why are their conversations and postcards always prefaced, and often monopolised, by 'what the weather is going to do'? These are important questions and our answers lead us to the very heart of the English condition. Accepting the cricket umpire's decision to stop play because of 'bad light', struggling for half an hour to be served in the scrum at a pub bar and stoically waiting on a train platform until 12.05 for the delayed 8.05 are all vital components of what it means to be English. Boredom? Insanity? Apathy? Not quite. It is of, course, that most under-rated of virtues: patience.

We also examine politics, the media, and the arts - all vital to a country's sense of worth, but never mind. English politicians invariably make headlines as a result of deviance far beyond that of Bill Clinton. Not only do MPs inhale, but they're usually wearing a plastic bag on their head at the time. The popular newspapers are full of naked breasts, and English art is symbolised by an unmade bed and a dead sheep in formaldehyde. On this evidence, is England a nation of pompous perverts who like staring at preserved sheep corpses? This hypothesis should not be dismissed out of hand.

The research for this book has taken many years and hundreds of miles, caused many wry smiles, frequent heartache and almost constant amazement. The patient English have, in short, been the source of frustration and hilarity in equal measure. Read on - the English may be patient, but they're never dull.

The Patient English - an indecipherable people. Until now.

Two: THE ROYAL FAMILY

The low-down on their Highnesses

The Royal Family is a fine institution, rather like a noble Victorian asylum. To understand the Royal Family is to understand the English, since it provides them with a sense of history and nationhood. It also reflects the change and uncertainty of the modern world, giving contrary England a sense of continuity. The English still look to the Royal Family to set the highest standards of etiquette, to undertake successful goodwill visits abroad and to open new hospital wings... its members have been exceptionally successful at opening new hospital wings.

Few other nations have royal families. The Russians murdered the Romanovs while America did not bother to establish one at all, wrongly believing that a President would prove less embarrassing as the nation's head of state. It is therefore no surprise that, in a world with few remaining hereditary monarchies, people should find the Windsors so peculiar. After all the English do - and they live with them.

The Royal Family has endured some dreadful publicity in recent times. The world's press pried incessantly into the Queen's *annus horribilis*. A similarly dreadful but shorter-lived disaster was Di Fortnight - the period of national hysteria following the death of Princess Diana. She was the only member of the Family who displayed any skills in the art of publicity. As a result, a republican thesis has gained a degree of popularity, arguing that the Royal Family is nothing more than a quite normally dysfunctional family which, without the glamorous and troubled Princess, appears staid and irrelevant. Perhaps they should be disbanded if they can't be more like her - dying young in car crashes.

This republicanism is complete nonsense, but is kept in check by English patience. There has always been a slow-burning revolutionary fuse in England, but it is so slow-burning it has never precipitated any great change. Renaming Di 'The People's Princess', for instance, is probably as close as the English will ever get to communism. This urge currently lives on with the 'chattering classes' - whom we shall meet in the following chapter, and they're rather too comfortable to set it off now. Meanwhile, the vast majority of the English remain devoted to the Royal Family - with an estimated eight in ten households possessing at least one commemorative royal wedding tea mug, which are mostly cracked, like the royal marriages themselves.

In this chapter, we try to ascertain the importance of this apparent anachronism, this throwback to an age of privilege and social hierarchy, which is still a fundamental part of the English national psyche. We meet the Windsors and reach the important conclusion that the Royal Family will remain in place for ever, if only because beheading is no guarantee of dislodging their crowns - hat pins don't y'know?

So who are the Royal Family and do they wear their crowns even when they are relaxing in front of the TV?

The Queen

Her Royal Highness, Her Majesty Queen Elizabeth II, is notable for being licked by the English general public thousands of times a day, and being fiddled with in their pockets as they fumble for loose change. In addition to stamps and coins, the Queen appears on the countless plaques and memorials unveiled by her in opening ceremonies, as well as on sundry household items which bear the small advert 'By Appointment to Her Majesty' - a reminder that she is available for children's parties, weddings, bar mitzvahs and funerals. In addition, the initials ER appear on all the post-boxes erected during her reign. ER stands for Elizabeth Regina, not emergency room in this case. In accordance with royal custom, and out of deference to his mother, Prince Charles prefaces everything he says with "Er".

Nominally, the Queen is the most important person in England, and accordingly holds many positions of responsibility. She is a devoted mother to her pet corgis, which depend on her for food and shelter, as do several ladies-in-waiting, numerous gardeners, a variety of cooks, cleaners and washers-up, a husband and great swathes of the English aristocracy. And she heads the Commonwealth (which means that their wealth is shared by her, not vice versa). Her Royal Highness is also the richest woman in England. She owns palaces, castles and Rolls Royces, thousands of acres of Britain and several further acres of hats. Her animal holdings include racehorses, Royal Swans, ducks, geese, herds of pigs and great swathes of the English aristocracy. Her collection of paintings includes numerous bad portraits of herself, and is priceless - though you can pick one up for a fiver.

Although Royal convention does not permit her to carry loose change or notes in her pockets or handbag, her monetary assets are huge. Some say that owning the Royal Mint is like a license to print money. She may not hold Queen Victoria's title 'Empress of India' - looking more like 'unimpressed of Windsor' most of the time - but she has her compensations. Three quarters of the globe may no longer be pink, but that same proportion of her enormous wardrobe most emphatically is.

Given the huge wealth at her disposal and the luxury in which she lives, one might ask why the Queen doesn't smile very much. Her expression, like the rest of her life, is governed by royal protocol. So, while it is true that her emotional range seems only to cover strained, and ever-so-slightly-amused, we can't presume to know that she is cold and unfeeling as a person. She may suffer from chronic flatulence for all we know, and the fact that we've never seen a footman's wig fly off in the blast could be testament to enormous reserves of physical, as opposed to emotional, repression. It would certainly explain why she spends so much time with horses. Or we may simply be dealing with the famous stiff upper lip of the aristocracy, of which more later. These are some theories explaining Her Majesty's stoic countenance, another brings us into contact with the other important members of the Royal Family.

Prince Charles

His Royal Highness, The Prince of Wales, is the King-in-Waiting and no fairy-tale Prince. In other words, the personification of the patient Englishman, waiting calmly for his mother to die before he can get on with his life. Waiting for him is a plum career, with a benefits package including the crown jewels and Buckingham Palace. Behind him are years of being groomed for the job - which explains that severe parting, anyway. He is ready to be King, wants to be King, is still waiting to be appointed King. But he must make do with his official title: 'His Royal Highness, The Prince of Wales'.

The Queen gave Wales to her eldest son as a twenty-first birthday present, and he has shown a particular fondness for it throughout his life, even going to the extreme length of learning to speak Welsh. It is an ancient tongue, which is exactly how yours feels after talking it. But it enables the Prince to converse with literally tens of his Welsh subjects, unfortunately covering the remaining three million with catarrh. Charles doesn't visit Wales often.

According to many Court correspondents and royal analysts, Prince Charles is a personable and talkative man. However, they point out that his personality took a severe battering during his school days. In keeping with the English aristocratic tradition of 'building character', Charles' mummy and daddy sent him to Gordonstoun, a 'progressive' public school in Scotland. Having been forced to take freezing cold baths at six o'clock every morning, sensitive Charles rapidly progressed into a nervous wreck. But he maintained a constantly stiff upper lip, and a general rigidity all over, which, alas, are there to this day.

The Prince's psychological instability manifested itself most obviously in his marital relations. Everyone said his union with Diana was a fairy-tale marriage, but, unlike a fairy-tale, it ended in a hideous nightmare. When it emerged that Charles had been carrying on a low key infatuation with Camilla Parker-Bowles, the nation was mystified. In all probability, this patient English love affair would have received a better reception if Charles had not been married to a minor deity at the time. However, in the years since Di Fortnight, public opinion towards Charles has mellowed. He may get his true sweetheart after all.

It is little wonder that Charles sometimes looks a little wistful, a little bored. He has waited half a lifetime for true love. And with his mother aiming to beat Victoria's record of sixty-four years on the throne, he might look a bit silly when, if ever, he becomes

King. It would be a huge embarrassment on his Coronation, if the entire nation were to giggle up its sleeve. An increasingly popular idea, therefore, is for the throne to skip a generation, like some unfortunate genetic trait, and pass to William. Quite how the country would deal with an ageing Charles bumbling around saying, "I could've been King you know?" is another matter. Probably in the same way that it now deals with the Queen Mother: Charles will become more loved than he ever would have been otherwise.

Princess Anne

Her Royal Highness, The Princess Royal, is the Queen's only daughter, and no fairy-tale Princess. Decidedly uncomfortable in traditional Princess attire, her preference for Barbour jackets and jeans, woollies and wellies makes her a fashion icon for farm labourers and abattoir workers. We all need our pin-ups, and this seems fair enough.

It wasn't fair enough for the Queen, however, who gave Anne the title of Princess Royal, as a reminder of the image she should be adopting. Anne accepted this with good grace but was reported privately to have said, "Princess Royal? What other bloody sort is there - a People's Princess?".

Princess Anne's forthright manner is in stark contrast to that of her reticent older brother. Her bossy and autocratic personality manifested itself as a child, and she bullied the already traumatised Charles mercilessly during school hols, pulling his pig tails 'til he screamed like a girl. Something similar caused the break-up of her marriage to Captain Mark Phillips.

The Queen's only daughter has therefore proved a constant worry - though none of the Royal Family criticises her, because she terrifies them all.

Prince Andrew

His Royal Highness, The Duke of York, is the Queen's second son and no fairy-tale Prince. He famously undertook a string of passionate and short-lived affairs during his long and sordid bachelorhood. His most notable mistress was the improbably named Koo Stark, a second rate soft porn star by profession. When the Duke of York finally decided to settle down, he chose to marry Sarah Ferguson - a second rate member of the upper-middle class by profession. This union was considered vulgar, crass and singularly inappropriate by his family. But she was warm, vivacious and open, so the public, of course, hated her. There's no pleasing some people.

After several acrimonious years of marriage they followed the well-established Royal precedent, and were divorced. When their joint bank accounts were examined by the lawyers, Her Royal ex-Highness is said to have exclaimed, "Oops. One appears to have spent a few million more than one thought one had!" In order to pay off her enormous debts, she became a television celebrity, advertising soft drinks, dietary products and appearing in the American sitcom, *Friends.* This admirable determination finally to pay her way was greeted with derision from all. There's no pleasing some people. The Queen was so appalled by this unseemly behaviour that she changed her wayward ex-daughter-in-law's official title from 'Her Royal Highness, the Duchess of York' to the somewhat plainer 'Fergie'.

Prince Edward

His Royal Highness, the Count of Wessex, is the Queen's third son and no fairy-tale Prince - well who is? The youngest and baldest of the Queen's sons has had a life dogged by uncertainty. There was uncertainty about his traditional youngest son position in the army, so he dropped out. There was uncertainty about his hair, so it dropped out. There was uncertainty about his sexuality, so he got married. He was certain that neither he, nor his fiancée, Sophie Rhys-Jones, would accept a title on their marriage, then they became the Count and Countess of Wessex. It is hoped that the general uncertainty about his life will cease now that he is married, and that his wife will help Edward to find himself. After all, don't you always find things down the back of the Sophie?

The Queen Mother

Her Royal Highness, Queen Elizabeth, is the Queen's mother, and, for once, is like a fairy-tale mother: manipulative and conniving. Unless she's died since publication, in which case she was a national treasure. When mentioning the Queen Mother, it is mandatory to follow her name with 'Gaw Blesser' (God Bless Her). This tabloid style of speech indicates that the Queen Mother is hugely popular with the public at large, who therefore have the right to patronise her horribly. This is quite apart from the fact that it's hard to see how Gaw could Blesser any further, short of rendering her immortal, Gaw Helpus. The Queen Mother's popularity is nearly as large as her debts, and is based on the fact that she was the King's wife, or Queen, when the Second World War was being fought. She regularly visited the smoking East End slums in the aftermath of blitzkrieg raids, offering regal sympathy to those whose lives lay in ruins, before returning to Buckingham Palace for crumpets and tea before a log fire. The working class appreciated these acts of selflessness even more when the palace itself was hit, and she made this speech:

"One has visited the East End, and one has seen the devastation - honestly, some of those houses look like a bomb's gorn orf. However, one doesn't really understand what one's unfortunate commoners... er, citizens... are going through, until one has been through it oneself. I'm sure you're all as devastated as one is that Buckingham Palace has been hit. But we shall not be moved, chiefly because the damage is miles away in another wing..."

She has remained popular ever since.

Apparently vulnerable, she is always lauded for her bravery through hip replacements, hypocrisy, gin drinking and placing duff bets on horses. It is possible that when she dies, the period of deep mourning may last as long as three weeks.

Prince Philip

His Royal Highness, the Duke of Edinburgh, is the Queen's husband. Royal protocol insists that the consort to the Queen must walk several paces behind her on all official business; he must defer to her decisions on all constitutional matters; and he must dutifully applaud when she unveils monuments or names ships. He has spent his entire adult life in the shadow of his wife - dependent upon her for his title and lifestyle. It is really not surprising that they are still married.

Philip's role is akin to that of an embarrassing old uncle. He relieves tiresome news of another Royal foreign tour with his singularly inappropriate remarks. His most notorious blunder came when he referred to the Japanese as 'slitty-eyed'. Whether this was the result of an ingenue-like ignorance of things Japanese, or of crass bad manners, the comment was viewed as 'unhelpful'.

But, just like an old buffer of an uncle, he gets away with it, causing amusement, shaking of heads, or even disgust back home - but never an international incident. Foreign dignitaries no doubt feel that it is an honour to be insulted by him, and if we could ask him why he behaves as he does, he would probably reply, "I'm a foreigner myself: no manners".

Princes William and Harry

We finally introduce the two Princes, William and Harry, who have the distinction of not (yet) bringing the monarchy into public disrepute. In private, they may well have pulled legs off spiders, relieved themselves in the woods or given each other Chinese burns, but these minor offences against propriety can be overlooked. Following Charles' ghastly schooling experiences, the Princes receive a relatively normal education. Not for them the progressive cold baths of Gordonstoun - they enjoy the luxury of traditional cold baths at Eton.

Popular opinion has it that William will make a good king, partly because of his father's likely advanced age by the time there is a vacancy on the throne and partly because he is handsome. The world loved his mother, and he looks so much like her that, before her death, she looked like him in drag. He has, therefore, become a pin-up for all right thinking middle-class girls, though poor old Harry is more of a pin-up for stick the tail on the donkey.

The very existence of the young Princes guarantees the future popularity of the Royal Family, and the pop-star hysteria that surrounds William will undoubtedly keep the republicans at bay for many a long year yet.

Bit parts

The Royal cast list extends further than this, of course. There are ever more improbably named Princesses such as Fergie's daughters, Beatrice and Eugenie, or Princess Michael of Kent, who is not half as masculine as she sounds. There are also various Viscounts, Earls and Duchesses, plus numerous foreign branches of the family. Some of these have celebrity status, but other than Lord Lichfield - who is famous as a photographer as well as a Royal - they are not worth mentioning. Even jilted rugby player's wives are celebrities these days, and being born sixty-fifth in line to the throne cannot compete with that.

The Future

Is it likely that the monarchy will be violently overthrown by bloody revolution? No. The revolutionaries in the chattering classes have done their bit by finally getting around to voting the Tories out of office, and that was only because they grew sick of the curtains at No. 10.

Is it likely, then, that the monarchy will be disbanded in sweeping constitutional change? Perhaps more so, but not for the foreseeable future. The English prefer to make the best of a bad job, and the drawback to constitutional change, as opposed to bloody revolution, is that the ex-Royal Family would still be alive and well and commanding as many column inches as before. The whole process would be devoid of point, and waste more money than the Queen can bring in via the tourist trade.

So the far-fetched pantomime that is the English monarchy looks set to continue. There is no rational justification for its existence, but which of us can claim that? Is it fair that such undemocratic privilege can still exist? Of course not, but remove the monarchy and people like Bill Gates will still walk this Earth - equally unfair, and not half as entertaining. The point of the Royal Family is precisely that they have no point. Pointless, unfair, hidebound, absurd, ridiculous, entertaining: these are exactly the qualities that make for that most elusive of things: the quintessentially English. However much of its unique identity England loses to rationalisation, let it not be its biggest and most glorious of absurdities: the Royal Family.

Three: SOCIAL CLASS

Knowing one's place

Former Prime Minister John Major is barely remembered, but when he is, it is for his idea of a 'classless society', although England's crumbling education system was probably not quite what he had in mind. What was happening in schools under his leadership mirrored developments in the country at large: the merging of everybody into one huge class. During the eighteen-year Conservative government, the old certainties of upper, middle and lower class were swallowed, to some extent, by an increasingly amorphous middle class. A thoroughly un-English trend, of course, and one which eventually saw Major voted out, his fantasy of a classless England dismissed by the vast majority of the class-obsessed English as the ravings of a madman.

Let's have a look at the four major areas of English society today: the upper, middle, working and under classes. We have already examined the Royal Family's untouchable status in English society. We now turn to their immediate social inferiors...

The aristocracy (upper class)

As a rule, only the aristocracy and the working class are truly content with their lot in life. The aristocracy has more reason to feel contented with its *modus vivendi* than its working-class counterpart, of course: aristocratic contentment comes with an unshakeable belief in the birthright of numerous extravagant privileges, riches and powers. There is a deep-seated satisfaction of the soul which comes from never having to do a lick of work for one's fortune, other than simply sitting back and inheriting it.

The aristocracy has always owned huge areas of Britain. For instance, the Sixth Duke of Westminster - Gerald Cavendish

Grosvenor to his friends - inherited one hundred thousand acres of land in Scotland and a sizeable chunk of Mayfair, one of the most exclusive and preposterously expensive areas of London. This makes him one of the richest aristocrats, but absolutely no fun at Monopoly.

Aristocratic well-being depends to a great extent on one's forebears. Very often, the young aristocrat will reach the end of a dissolute youth spent gambling on cards and stocks, imbibing all sorts of exotic drugs and generally living it up, ready for a nice cosy inheritance to wrap himself in. What does he find? That his forebears have carelessly frittered it all away gambling on cards and stocks, imbibing all sorts of exotic drugs and generally living it up, leaving him with a vast acreage of Scotland. This does provide an income, but it's immediately sucked into the upkeep of numerous mouldering castles, and to whom can you sell one hundred thousand acres of Scotland? The picture of it would never fit in the estate agent's window for a start.

There are ways around this financial embarrassment, however. One is the dreaded work. Luckily, the aristocrat has an unerring ability to find positions of remuneration in English boardrooms. When word escapes of an aristocrat's availability for part-time employment, representatives of English blue-chip companies immediately form an orderly queue on the gravel forecourt of said mouldering pile, and patiently wait their turn to offer him lucrative directorships. The aristocrat usually chooses those positions which do not demand his actual attendance at the tedious meetings - putting one's feet up on the boardroom table does scuff the shoe leather so.

The damp and draughty old mansions themselves have proved to be another money-spinner for the aristocracy. Cluttered with ornaments, suits of armour, paintings, armour, suits of armour, sculptures and arbours, the patient English middle classes are happy to spend their hard-earned money and precious spare hours visiting the treasure troves of their social superiors, keeping them in the lifestyle to which every middle-class man and woman would like to become accustomed.

From early in life, the members of this class are taught that they are the natural social leaders of England. Not for nothing is the aristocracy referred to as 'society' - a term which relegates everyone else to hoi polloi. The working class have had a long and close association with the aristocracy, working for them as servants and tenants, and the underclass have traditionally been booted out of their meagre homes and thrashed by them for poaching. Therefore, these two classes have an inbuilt disdain for their social betters and are likely to fall about laughing should an aristocrat speak to them. But the remainder of the English feel an acute sense of social inadequacy, awe and respect when addressed by a gent - the effect of his good breeding causes constant frustration and humiliation as they try to ape the aristocrat's carefree insouciance. They will always fail, though, because such carefree insouciance comes from the natural assumption that one is simply better than everyone else.

The aristocrat's unnerving ability to dress immaculately for every occasion also deeply affects the middle classes. There is something about a middle-class man in his rarely worn dinner suit - the stumbling gait and glassy expression owe nothing to inebriation and everything to a mix of self-consciousness and misplaced pride. By contrast, the aristocrat is as comfortable in his own tailored dinner suit as he is wearing his one hundred per cent cashmere pyjamas.

As for table manners, the aristocracy are not just born with a silver spoon in their mouth; they know which spoon it is, too. Their ability with cutlery is innate and thoughtless. The middle classes, on the other hand, hanker for an understanding of table manners but constantly trip over their own misconceptions. They have added extra impediments for themselves by inventing fish knives and dessert forks and sundry other useless implements which an aristocrat would no more recognise than they do. In fact, everyone but the middle classes sit down at the dinner table to *eat*, employing whatever means at their disposal to fill their bellies, be it a hundred kitchen staff and twenty six pantries, or enough lard to pan-fry a whale. Only the middle classes are too busy with their cutlery to remember to enjoy their food. All a bit of a sham really, but it hardly stops these aspirants from thinking they are being 'posh' and 'doing the right thing' - both points of constant reassurance to the English middle classes.

An English aristocrat's birth is accompanied by the bestowal of a title such as Viscount, Earl, Marquess or Lord - a symbol of difference handed down over centuries to separate him from the lower orders of society, whose ancestors didn't please Good Queen Bess by trimming their beards before a bit of gratuitous arse-licking. The infant aristocrat's sense of superiority is reinforced by the fact that he doesn't have parents, but staff. His every whim is catered for by a nanny, butler, various cooks and a miscellany of other domestic servants. Eventually the valet and the equerry become the most important underlings in the life of the male aristocrat, while the ever-dependable ladies-in-waiting become vital to the female variety.

During his formative years, the youngster develops his natural arrogance and an expectation that all should defer to him. It is important that he learns this well, for a strange day is coming:

"Lay out my sailor suit for me Nanny, there's a good woman. Think we'll dispense with the hat, though, don't you? It's inclined to make one look like a siss... I say! Who the Hell are you?"

"I'm your Mummy, darling."

"My what!"

"Your Mummy. I've come to wish you farewell."

"But you've only just got here. Where are you going?"

"You are going, my dear Cadwallon, to school. One of the best public schools in the country, as it happens."

"I'm not mixing with the damn public!"

"No, that's right, with little boys just like you."

"Oh my God!"

So now comes the real test for our representative toff, little Cadwallon. His parents, busy with their important social obligations of hosting society dinners, attending society dinners and arranging future society dinners, can do without a precocious brat under their feet. The phrase 'Children should be seen and not heard' is a middle class mantra. The upper class don't even like to see theirs, except on special occasions - Christmas Day, Easter Sunday and from a distance at school functions. At boarding school, Cadwallon will have to do his best to survive among several hundred other young brats, all trying to impose their will on each other, if not their willies. As men, they will wear their old school ties with pride, happily forgetting (or happily remembering, if the perversion takes hold) that Lord Plankton-Cribbage used it to drag them screaming round the fives court when they were nine.

And so the round of prep-schools, housemasters, dorms and studies is endured - any kinks and flaws in Cadwallon's nature being ironed out and replaced with new ones - until, at eighteen, off he goes to Oxford or Cambridge.

During his university career, the aristocrat remains aloof from the other classes that have 'invaded' these seats of learning in recent times. He mixes only with his fellow aristocrats, smokes only luxury Turkish cigarettes and Cuban cigars and drinks only the finest vintages:

"Mine's a large port, Stivvings."

"Really old man? Me too: Papa owns Southampton."

On the academic front, the aristocrat hardly wishes to shame the family by failing outright, but sees no reason to interrupt his frequent coffee mornings, cocktail parties and balls for such base and unsociable activities as serious study. A class of degree, the 'recommended pass', has been developed specifically for him. This allows the university authorities to award a degree because the aristocratic candidate sounds like he should have passed - and because his family funds the scholarships for those in less esteemed social positions.

Upon completion of his formal education, the aristocrat returns to the family seat, taking charge of some of its affairs. Spending the family money on crashing classic cars, starting fist fights in fashionable restaurants and taking extended holidays in exotic air stewardesses are examples of this new-found sense of responsibility. Much time will be spent in London socialising 'at the club'. The club in this context is a gentleman's club, not a bingo hall or British Legion.

During his time in London, it is absolutely vital that the aristocrat attends the various engagements of 'the season', or 'summer', as everyone else calls it. Balls, garden parties and picnics are intrinsic rituals of the season. In addition, the Henley Regatta, Royal Ascot and Wimbledon provide pleasant opportunities to appreciate sporting endeavour, whilst drowning in Pimms and gorging on fresh strawberries. This social whirl supplies Cadwallon with ideal opportunities for putting himself about with debs. In this context, debs is not some hideous lower-middle-class sales rep, but short for 'debutantes'. These young ladies have been bred specially and slightly matured for eighteen years, which is when they 'come out'. This simply means that they have come of age, not that they declare themselves lesbians: leave that to the ungentlemanly gents they refuse to sleep with. Eventually, however, an appropriate union will be arranged - once the family has seen off the lower-middle-class sales rep. called Debs. This is a 'match' made with a peer, and not under one. The chance of locating a wife is improved dramatically should the aristocrat demonstrate a facility in the game of polo, as female members of the elite are traditionally attracted to those who can ride a horse and wield a stick simultaneously.

But let's take Cadwallon back a few years. He is eight, and experiencing difficulties at boarding school thanks to that business with Gramcock Minor's bottom and the sardines. He is being mercilessly bullied by Gramcock Senior and his cronies, who leave slugs in his underwear, set fire to his bed and whip him with copies of Country Living and Penthouse. Cadwallon's fling with Gramcock Senior is a few years hence, so Cadwallon is obviously ecstatic when the holidays begin and he can rest his weary buttocks at the country seat. Unfortunately, holidays always come to an end. On his last evening at home, Cadwallon is in the East Wing, knocking on his father's study door. He waits for the regulation four and a half minutes, then enters, approaching his father's leather chair via the rose arbour (the direct route). Cadwallon is doing his best to control his emotions as he faces his father's stern visage. Alas, he is unfamiliar with the old chap and is actually facing the stern visor of a suit of armour. When his father coughs behind him, Cadwallon turns in surprise and a solitary tear begins its slow trickle down his cheek. Father's expression immediately blackens:

"Come, come, this won't do, no, no, stiff upper lip, what?"

This reassures Cadwallon hugely, and, bidding his father goodnight, he turns to leave with an upper lip like a starched collar. Unfortunately, the bottom one is flapping about as if caught in a sudden gale.

The English inability, or rather disinclination, to show emotion is firmly embedded in the traditions of the upper class - and the rest of English society follows. It has been noted correctly that the English are a repressed people, who generally feel acute embarrassment when witnessing their fellows acting in an honest and open manner. The English often suffer dizzy spells when they come across a public 'scene' - a couple arguing in the supermarket, for example, or a vicar masturbating in the belfry. The feeling that public displays of emotion are 'bad form' has been handed down from the aristocracy, whose independence cannot allow for 'weaknesses' which might be exploited by the unscrupulous. Their most basic maxim of behaviour is 'the stiff upper lip'. (Not to be confused with the cause of most of those lesbian jibes about the debs.)

And on we blunder. If Cadwallon is lucky, his parents will die while he is relatively young, leaving him the family fortune, and that ever useful independence and emotional constipation:

"Why aren't you going to your parents' funeral, Cadwallon?"

"Come off it, Nanny, I hardly knew them."

Few tourists will ever meet Cadwallon: they may pay a tenner to visit his house, but he won't be there. The house is stuffed with artefacts that long ago ceased to have any practical or aesthetic use, such as chamber pots and candlesticks, obsolete since the invention of running water and electricity. Meanwhile, Cadwallon is sitting in a nearby hostelry, indistinguishable from the locals in a vast jumper apparently knitted from his beard. So never let it be said that the English stately home is full of potties - they're all getting pissed in the pub.

The middle class

This is the most diverse and amorphous class in England - a shifting, frustrated and restless entity, like The Blob in a cardigan. Its members are constantly striving to climb the social ladder. Occasionally, individual members of the middle class are able to ingratiate themselves with the aristocracy. This is especially the case when 'new' money or new genes are needed to inject life blood into an ailing noble line - usually via the unpalatable media of matrimony or kidnapping. Conversely, it is possible for members of the middle class to fall from their middle-ranking position in society into the underclass, particularly if they offend the local Conservative Women's Society. Moreover, individuals are able to alter their position within the middle class itself. For instance, a particularly successful member of the lower-middle class can leapfrog the middle-middle class and join the *nouveau riche* within a generation, should his chain of sex boutiques or organ farms increase their annual profit margins for long enough. However, the *nouveau riche* is not to be confused with the upper-middle class, which is like a miniature aristocracy with pretensions. Some of these families are just as long-lived as the aristocracy, but were never good enough at toadying to receive titles.

While it would be unfair to say that the rest of the middle classes are bastards, there is an insecurity and flux characterising their existence which makes their lineage uncertain. For instance, a contemporary member of the middle class might feasibly trace his line back to the working class - a thoroughly annoying eventuality since the aim is to trace your family back to nobility. Genealogy is a common middle class hobby. Its jackpot is the discovery that a great-great-uncle several times removed, was the disgraced son of a lesser Duke, from whom one can claim blue blood.

Many representatives of the middle class are extremely wealthy in their own right. Some toil in the City of London, as stockbrokers or traders on the money markets. Senior lawyers, accountants and doctors generate enormous fees as a result of their professional standing. These members of the middle class can therefore afford gigantic and luxurious homes, keep several thoroughbred horses and mistresses and buy large yachts or small islands. But the important distinction to make here is a simple one: their riches are *nouveau*. These members of the middle class have had to work hard to make their fortunes, and they are not ashamed of it. The aristocracy has a disdain for money engendered by the fact that it flows hot and cold from their taps. In lieu of titles other than derogatory French ones like *nouveau riche* and *bourgeois*, the middle class chases wealth, in the belief that it will make them better people. However, despite the ability of the *nouveau riche* to compete financially with the upper class, it cannot compete with the aristocratic ability to sit in a rambling country house for years on end, doing absolutely nothing.

Those within the highest stratum of the middle class send their children to the best boarding schools and attend the season's delightful events. Yet no matter how much they spend on the catering arrangements for their summer garden party, no matter how many old masters they hang in their downstairs loo, they remain excluded from the highest rank and, as such, can never attain true equality with their blue-blooded social superiors. This is perhaps why they are so tight-arsed and mean spirited.

As we shift our gaze from the monied sub-category of the middle class, we are immediately earholed by the 'chattering classes'. Not so much a category of class, as an affliction of too much education and comfort, chatterers make a habit of talking about the important issues of the day with considerable gravity, passion and, sometimes, knowledge. Their occupations - in the media, the arts, advertising or teaching, for example - give them an inflated sense of their own importance and encourage them to chatter inordinately. They earn less money than the *nouveau riche*, but find 'fulfilment' from their interesting careers, rather than from fiddling their clients' accounts or extracting their wisdom teeth.

Chatterers put great store in their (self-induced) position as outsiders - although feeling uncomfortable with one's surroundings is a classic middle-class trait - and take a dim view of everyone else. This is chiefly because everyone else is unable to see the truth: that the middle class is soulless; advertising is an art-form; accountants are pompous dullards; talk is cheap; conversation is enriching; that 'they' ought to do something and that it's frustrating living in a country where less respect and admiration are given to independent thought than a country house and title.

In numerical terms, the sub-strata examined above are relatively small, but the middle of the middle class is enormous. Forming the truly spineless backbone of England, the middle-middle class is aptly, and disparagingly, termed 'Middle England' by the chattering classes. Its representatives live comfortably, filling their spare time with gardening and DIY. They spend their entire lives trying to emulate the traditions and mannerisms of the aristocracy, but are by and large unsuccessful, except when it comes to sexual deviance, at which they're quite good. During dinner parties, the middle-middle class insists upon the observance of the rules of dining etiquette: soup must be spooned away from the diner and bread must not be thrown in to make 'ducks'. The idea of making ducks would never even occur to the well-bred aristocrat, and if it did, he'd probably think it a jolly, jolly wheeze, but denial of these simple pleasures is a sacrifice indeed for the middle-middle class.

In place of the priceless pieces of art kept by the aristocracy, worthless pieces of tat clutter the houses of the middle-middle class. Worthless, but not cheap. Ever wondered who buys the hand-crafted commemorative plates that are advertised in Sunday supplements? The interior of the home is regularly dusted and cleaned, in case visitors call unexpectedly. If they do, exclamations of "You must excuse the mess" and "What a state we're in" fill the air like spray polish. The walls hang with gilt and guilt.

Slipping further down the greasy pole of the English social hierarchy, we find the lower-middle class. Its members are less financially comfortable, because they've spent their hard-earned wages on consumer trappings like satellite dishes, and less obsessively fastidious, so they don't mind the extra cables hanging all over their house.

At the lower-middle class dinner table, Mother spends her entire meal watching for lapses in her children's standards of etiquette - elbows on the table, chips up the nose and so on.

"Posh children never stick chips up their nose, Terry."

Which is true, they use asparagus tips instead.

On the linguistic front, she castigates her offspring's tendency to drop letters.

"I 'ate me peas!", exclaims Terry, earning a slap round the head.

"You don't 'ate peas, Terry. You hate them."

"No, I've finished."

"In which case," (slap), "I ate *my* peas."

The constant fight to maintain standards is exhausting and dispiriting for the lower-middle class mother, which explains the high sales of cheap white wine amongst this class - a beverage to which she often turns for solace.

Such rules and regulations - diluted versions of the aristocratic ideal - are the bedrock of lower-middle class existence. Only by slavishly aping the behaviour of the highest class, its members believe, can they possibly avoid being called 'common'. This label implies a complete lack of breeding, good taste and manners - in other words the ideals of the working class, sitting in uncomfortably close proximity on the social scale.

The working class

Traditionally, hardness was the mainstay of urban working-class life: hard graft, hard skin; hard drinking, hard arteries; hard religion, hard hearts. Hardiness was manliness, and that went for the women too. And this hardness was kept through the generations with jealous pride: there was no middle-class desire for social climbing. Woe betide any working class son, trying to buck the system, coming home with tales of his first day as a clerk.

"Look, Dad, my first industrial injury!"

"Where?"

"Look there, a paper cut!"

"Paper cut! PAPER CUT! You soft bastard, I'll give you paper cut!"

"Oo, don't, they sting like hell... Is me Mam in? Brought home me underpants for her to wash."

"Quite right too, washing pants is woman's work."

"I'll say, nearly sprained me wrist wringing a pair out."

A son like this would be suspected of homosexual tendencies, certainly, and might possibly be accused of the far worse crime of 'class treachery'. Although an aristocrat fraternising in the lower classes might just have this accusation levelled at him, it is really a working class phenomenon, which springs directly from the selfish fear of seeing one's offspring escape drudgery.

Where does this masochistic work ethic come from? From above, of course: God (the factory boss). It was in the interests of the owners of pits, mills and factories, to keep their workers on their knees even when they weren't at work. Fear of hellfire and brimstone for eternity provided a staff and a rod, with which workers were beaten everyday of their lives - convinced it was better to suffer on Earth than in the hereafter as well. Thus, many industrial towns were built upon pork-piety: the wealth of reverent men and the backs of their God-fearing workers.

Every now and then the workers would strike. This is as close to revolution as the English ever came, and it suited their temperament because they could stand in a line and drink tea. It also weeded out the class traitor, the social aspirant who would rather work for money than class ethics. "Looking after your own" was the mantra. "Support your class" the strikers cried - unless your family got in the way, then your class could sod off.

Money was relatively unimportant to the working-class bloke, which was just as well. He earned just enough to pay for the roll-up cigarettes and the pies and chips which formed his staple diet. To complete the working-class lifestyle of wearing out one's kneecaps before the age of forty, there was the pub. Here, the workers would go to take the weight off their knees by falling on their faces, having drunk fifteen pints of beer and ten whiskies.

More traditional still, were the rural working class, for whom hardness was also the mainstay of life: hard land, hard tools; hard churning, hard cheese; hard cider, hard heads. The main difference between the urban and rural working classes was that where the former were ruled by the middle class playing God, the latter were ruled by the aristocracy playing God. Wealthy land owners would lord it over their labourers - what else can one do, when one is actually a Lord? To complete this incubus-like role, the aristocracy would sometimes take a farmer's child into 'service'. So instead of going up factory, a yokel would go up big house, or up Lady of big house, if he became a gamekeeper.

Because the servant class was regarded as a specialised section of the working class, going into service was not regarded as class treachery. And as far as the aristocracy were concerned, taking servants fulfilled the requirements for butlers, housemaids, stablemen and the legitimate need for illegitimate babies (new blood don't y' know?).

Both the urban and rural working class were duly deferential to their superiors, or betters; caps were doffed, forelocks tugged and curtsies curtseyed. The average working-class Englishman had no ambition to escape from his unsophisticated lifestyle and felt under no pressure to speak properly - he was rightly proud of his strong and incomprehensible dialect. He was a common man, with common tastes, and was perfectly happy to remain in this lowly position until the inevitable fatal coronary at the age of fifty-seven.

And all of this still holds true. Recently, however, this class has contracted, as the closure of England's coal mines, shipyards, and steel foundries has robbed the urban working class of its defining feature: work. They never had much class to begin with and they have now become the urban unemployed. Some of the rural working class scrape a living as tour guides in stately homes, though BSE has killed off most of their employers. Thus, an abyss has opened below the working class. Never traditionally aspirant, the working class has its pride, and dreads the slide into the underclass (see below).

Ironically, service has proved to be their escape. Not service to the aristocracy, but to things. Nobody in England produces anything anymore, they just look after things. This is called 'the service industry', and most people are in it. Therefore, those of the working class who do work are now middle class, in terms of wealth and occupation, but they have none of the middle class guilt or hang ups about propriety, which is why you see more people in vests and track suits these days. Hence New Labour, which is like Old Labour, but without the labouriousness of actually working hard for a living.

Rejoice in the birth of a bland new swathe of middle class drones. Old working class die-hards are finding that they *are* dying hard, if they don't embrace the soft new world being carefully made-over for them. And with the pitiful level of the dole these days, they realise there's no choice between a job centre and a call centre.

The underclass

Having grown so quickly during the Eighties, the underclass is in something of a unique position in relation to its counterparts, which have been established for many centuries. Margaret Thatcher really only began to mould today's underclass twenty years ago, when she decided to close England's factories and mines - thus destroying working class work, way of life and pride. A new stratum was created... and neglected. Although, as we've seen, there is a new option for the ex-working class, it has only really been chosen by the younger generation. Some of the previous generation renounced everything that was good about their working class roots and simply lingered in the hard bits.

Those of the underclass lucky enough to have a home live on council estates - an area of public land and housing, carefully avoided by all but those who live there, the police and social services. These estates were built for working men and their families - the idea being that the men would be away at work and too tired to beat up the missus when they came in. Robbed of work, the men laze around at home providing BO, bad influence and black eyes. Elsewhere, the average middle class street will have its fair share of hedgehogs or foxes roaming during the night. In stark contrast, whatever time of day or night, the council estate is besieged by packs of vicious and angry dogs, second only to packs of vicious and angry kids.

The underclass wear their hearts on their sleeves... well, on their skin actually, along with numerous other tattoos. Ex-prisoners, for instance, favour swallows. Indeed, swallows outnumber dogs on many estates. Neo-nazism is rife among this class, and you can spot a neo-nazi because his political opinions are literally written all over his face. Tattoo artists are the most literary, even literate, people on most estates.

Other members of the underclass live in swanky, big city buildings, or at least in the doorways of swanky, big city buildings. Although excellent schemes are afoot to help the homeless, it's only possible to buy *The Big Issue* once, so middle class guilt is also on the increase. Some simply scoff, "Oh I never give to beggars, they only spend it on booze and fags anyway" as they sip another G&T and light a cigar. Which of us wouldn't turn to booze and fags in such a hopeless position?

So-called 'new-age travellers' provide more exotic specimens of the underclass. Having given up on class altogether to attain spiritual enlightenment, they transport a motley collection of old buses around the countryside, almost as if it were a free country. This infuriates the middle classes, of course, who are secretly insanely jealous, and stop them from parking whenever they can.

Conclusion

True class distinctions are more a product of the mind than circumstance, and probably the middle class mind at that. This is why class will continue in England until the bourgeoisie fall in bloody revolution, or run out of new wallpapering ideas. Class then is at the heart of Englishness and England probably enjoys more class than is strictly necessary.

Four: THE PUBLIC HOUSE

I am what I drink - and I am a bitter man

The Royal Family and the various gradations of class are an important part of England's national character. But were they to disappear, it is just possible that England would find the will to carry on - probably with the aid of a stiff drink down the local. If the English woke up to a world without public houses, however, it is likely that England would simply collapse.

Following an arduous day at work (or the benefits office), the majority of the English like to spend their evenings in the pub, delighting in rituals unchanged for generations (many of these previous generations can still be seen propping up the bar). Exceptions to this rule include the Royal Family, although Prince Philip has been known to spend an evening or two in the Queen's Arms. Middle class women are also rarely spotted in the public house, preferring to keep their alcoholism a private matter (and are therefore watered as often as the middle class lawn).

To the uninitiated, the pub's intricate system of conventions can be frustrating and daunting, but careful study brings its own very great rewards.

The pub is the natural setting for the repressed Englishman because he is allowed to stray from the humdrum - but not too far - via a series of compelling polarities: escape and familiarity; license and licensing laws; cheese and onion. Barstools, banter and barmaids help the Englishman unwind, while he indulges his patience waiting twenty minutes for a drink. Furthermore, being ordered home every night at the same time by the same patronising landlord fits in perfectly with the Englishman's love of routine and his deferential world-view. Indeed, no other institution comes so close to responding to the nation's love of order and fear of change.

Rules of the house

As the term implies, any member of the public is welcome in the public house, so long as he respects the rules laid down by the pub in question. The English refer to those who drink in the public house as 'punters'. Here are some of the rules which punters need to look out for.

Some pubs do not tolerate 'foul and abusive language' from their punters, but such places are few and far between. Indeed, many pubs have a tradition of English vernacular which is positively mediaeval, with entire conversations based on no more than six or seven choice expletives. Disgusting language and crude comments are really only discouraged in the new 'family pubs'. The irony is that with hordes of sweating children darting between the tables, upsetting drinks and regulars in equal measure, the family pub is far more likely to inspire angry profanity among its punters than any other.

Certain pubs operate strict dress policies - non-negotiable dress codes - summarised by the 'NO JEANS, NO TRAINERS' or 'SMART DRESS ONLY' signs hanging outside. Pubs displaying these signs are guarded by at least two steroid-pumped bouncers bent on refusing entrance - because to admit passing trade is to admit failure. The most insignificant sartorial oversight can provide the bouncer with a valid reason for exclusion. The reveller may be wearing a Gucci shirt, Armani trousers and Calvin Klein underpants. But if there is a hint of denim, the bouncer manfully struggles to articulate, "No jeans", and will fail to be swayed by rational argument, agonised pleas or even bribes. "No jeans", he might repeat as often as twice, before ending the argument by standing on the complainant's throat.

Of course, the 'NO JEANS, NO TRAINERS' rule has a historical pedigree. The public house is a traditional home for spontaneous bare-knuckle fighting. Over the centuries, landlords found that punters were less inclined to indulge in pugilism when dressed in their Sunday best. Until recently, jeans and sneakers were not a punter's most valued clothes. But now that these items cost more than your average three piece suit, the rule seems a little anachronistic. As yet, this development has had little impact on the 'NO JEANS' policies.

Many pubs bear a sign reading: 'NO INDUSTRIAL CLOTHING', which suggests that a punter wearing heavily soiled overalls and boots may not be welcome. This, in all its true English absurdity, rarely means that he will not be served or made to feel entirely welcome. Rather that he is not allowed into the 'lounge' area of the bar, populated by the middle classes. The 'tap room' - or 'spit and sawdust' as they're sometimes known, due to the choice of drinks on offer - welcomes the workman with open arms. There he is provided with the ten pints of warm bitter required to lubricate his larynx after a hard day's shouting from scaffolding.

England boasts several particular types of public house. Some of these provide an intoxicating atmosphere of English eccentricity, while others provide a sobering reminder that England has some severe social problems. Let us see which is which.

The traditional country pub

As the name suggests, this is the oldest type of watering-hole in England, with a timeless and archaic quality. Low oak beams, installed long before the advent of health and safety officers, but shortly after shipwrecks, jut boldly from the ancient ceiling. These are rendered less dangerous by the thick, centuries-old smog of pipe smoke that cushions the cranium in the collisions that occur to and from the bar. But in these comfortable, dark, nostalgic places, there are other areas of danger - the ale for starters.

The traditional country inn takes pride in England's past and its hand-pumped beers resonate with centuries of overindulgence. *Old Squirrel's Todger* and *Strumpet's Fart* are but two of a myriad of brand names which have beguiled the imagination and turned the stomach of punters over the years. Their continued popularity illustrates the English punter's fidelity to tradition and his discerning, but unsophisticated palate:

"Tastes loike piss to me, Amos."

"Ar, could be Clem, but be that badger's piss, or stoat?"

The punter drinks mostly to forget. In here the first thing he may want to forget is imminent death by a falling trusking fork, or any of the baroque assortment of obsolete farming tools that dangle precariously from the walls and ceiling.

A museum's worth of bent poking-Jills, twisted jizzock harnesses and burnt frumpty tins hang from every available surface, defying category and gravity alike. Acknowledging England's agricultural heritage is one thing, but one must be careful - an ancient urinal mistaken for a rustic cider flagon is lavatorial history beyond the pail. Still, these artefacts are preferable to the modern alternatives: rotting Tupperware and plastic repro. soap ads. Any yokel will tell you that genuine shit is better than sham poo.

In addition to providing bevies of beverages, the traditional country pub offers a range of food. The menu details the availability of 'traditional fayre'. This translates as 'past its sell-by date'. The convention of serving unpleasant meals is justified on historical grounds: 'This pie has been reheated and served since Tudor times'. To eat one is to indulge in a little history ... and relive the plague.

More of the country pub - the quintessential English social institution - later. Suffice to say here that it is the grandfather of the English pub community. Like most grandfathers, it may be unfashionable, open to ridicule and smell funny, but it holds an unmatched position in the nation's heart. Still flourishing in every corner of England's green and pleasant land are hostelries, green and unpleasant, like Plantagenet cheese - and just as durable. May they last forever.

The Irish theme pub

The pub boasting a Gaelic theme has become increasingly popular in England during recent times. An explanation for this is that England's own popular culture is based upon vitriolic xenophobia and failed imperialism. To base a public house on this theme would be as dismal as to base a country on it. In any case, people go to the pub to escape their humdrum normality. Hence the arrival of the Irish theme pub, which bares no relation to real life of any kind, even that of the Irish. Irish culture is based on folk bands, excessive drinking, and banter - 'the crack'. In the early 1990s, several breweries realised the Irish could have something there. Replace the folk music with The Corrs, pump in crude oil and call it stout, show football on a big screen and it just might work.

Due credit must go, therefore, to the credulity of the English punter, for the Irish theme pub is still unfathomably popular - offering all the benefits of an Irish pub, without the Irish. And why are there no Irish? Because they can't find their way out of Ireland - some English divil has taken down all their road signs to hang on the walls of his pub.

The chain pub

Having witnessed the popularity of Irish theme pubs, corporate breweries have tried to create other variations on the theme, each as hideous as the next. This is their attempt at the English theme pub. As a result this once idiosyncratic and individual institution has been moulded into many different styles of homogenous chain: the laddish, beery chain with the wacky pub names; the after office hours, art-noveau mish mash, which mocks the illiteracy of the management glitterati with jumble sale books round the walls; the cosmopolitan life-in-a-big-city chain, where excitement means paying through the nose for dry white, and talking out of the arse for dry wit. And for each of these a cheaper, nastier imitator. Then there are the myriad family chains, which regrettably have a section of their own, below.

The racket from all these chains is like a thousand Jacob Marleys haunting every neighbourhood, for many is the fine old pub which has undergone an eerie transformation at the hands of corporate greed. Punters' memories of broken agricultural tools and eclectic bitters become mingled with bottled lager and mirrored walls. The English believe that the chain pub is threatening the eccentric soul of the nation's pub industry, and traditionalists rightly view this development with concern.

The family pub

Before some cretin coined the term 'family pub', a family pub either served the feudal village near a country estate - 'The Duke of Thrombosis Arms' - or a local tavern where three generations of peasant might drink, fart and fight together - 'The Flea Skinner's Arms'. Or both.

Unfortunately, it now means the alcoholic equivalent of McDonalds, with a children's menu of *Cheeky Chicken Nuggets* and *Bonkers Baked Beans*, coupled with a supervised children's play area which even matches the beer for hideous plasticity. This keeps the kiddies close at hand for every moment of mummy and daddy's marital breakdown.

The family pub is therefore a crass compromise between a pub, designed for drinking; a restaurant, designed for eating; and a kindergarten, designed to house children (while adults go out and do adult things, like drink in a pub, or eat in a restaurant). The revolting smell of juvenile sweat and the grating sound of immature screams are nearly as bad as those in the chain pubs.

Punters used to go to pubs to escape their families. Now they are lumbered with everybody else's, too. The rise of the family pub is a cause of national shame

The down-at-heel-pub

Down-at-heel pubs, or 'dives', are one of the last bastions of unspoilt English pub culture, and are thus ideal for the serious tourist wishing to study the real life of these islands. Whole new sub-strata of the class system are revealed within, from working class, through criminal class, to dregs-of-humanity. Also on display are such genuine artefacts of English pub culture as the surly landlord, ash covered tables and peanuts whose price is anything but peanuts.

Full of colourful characters - so called because of their tattoos - the dive offers a warm welcome to the visitor. Friendly guides will immediately inquire as to the visitor's interests with, "Wotchoo you lookin' at?". The savvy tourist must show that he is streetwise to the concerns of his host. "It's all right, I'm not a plain clothes policeman" is the recommended reply. Mindful of his manners, the guide might next politely enquire, "Are you taking the piss?" This is their slang for, "Would you like a drink?" It would be rude to refuse. "Yes, I'd love a glass, thank you," should suffice. At this point, the visitor usually receives his glass, at great velocity. Service is second to none in the dive.

The pub with a beer garden

As its name implies, this category of pub offers the punter an opportunity to drink outside - a practice followed religiously by the English during the summer season (12th -15th July). If the sun appears during this season, every beer garden in the country is immediately filled with eager punters keen to achieve the continental look (lobster thermidor and a glass of lager).

Most beer gardens boast a variety of plants and flowers which have been thoroughly watered through the seasons with discarded ale. The alcoholic pollen attracts special varieties of bee and wasp who intoxicate themselves and somehow always manage to end up in the punter's pint glass. The helpful landlord is always at hand, though, to provide anaesthetic in the form of horizontal lubricant. After third degree burns and insect bites, excessive consumption is the only viable antidote.

Despite this variety of pubs and their vastly differing clientele, their highly-detailed conventions dictate the conduct of the punter is the same in all. Ex-con or rich financier, it matters not, the rules do not change. Pub conventions have a long, distinguished and unalterable pedigree, far removed from the contingent nature of everyday modern life.

The punter's initial concern has always been how to get served. This is not an idle question. The motivation to drink becomes a consuming passion for many Englishmen as the evening draws on. Unfortunately, actually purchasing a drink can be fraught with difficulty. Let's look at two case studies for enlightenment on this issue.

1. The busy chain pub

During peak drinking hours in any such pub in the land, liquid relief lies beyond a throbbing mass of humanity, packed into a small section of the pub, known as the bar.

The English pub has no concept of waiter service and only a scant notion of bar service. The punter is expected to do all the hard work - elbowing total strangers to get to the bar, catching the attention of the bar steward, making himself heard ('No! BRANDY and SODA, not SHANDY and CIDER'), then renegotiating the masses with armfuls of drink, while the pub staff remain safely ensconced behind the bar.

The novice punter, inexperienced in the strange ways of the pub, can expect to experience mild frustration, intense jealousy and psychotic anger. During particularly busy periods (11am until 11pm), the wait to be served can appear an entirely hopeless mission. In such a situation, one's patience towards English eccentricity can be severely tested.

How can this happen - and how is it possible to avoid such a volatile reaction to the spiritual home of the English?

The pub, it should be noted, does not operate the ticket system, found for instance, at the delicatessen of a local supermarket. This system guarantees fair service: expecting to be served in order, people then queue up properly, united against their common foe, the ticket machine. The pub is similar, except that the common foe for the punter is not the ticket machine, but the other punters. Stratagems and ruses are therefore required which are, ironically, so unsportsmanlike (and sometimes downright brutal) that most Englishmen need a stiff drink before they can put them into practice properly.

Predicting potential spaces opening in the scrum is crucial. Competition for these precious spaces is intense, and the penalties for leaping into an occupied space can be severe. One tactic is to tap the chap in front and, in friendliest brogue, say, "Excuse me". Few Englishmen will fail to respond with, "Certainly". Offer up a "Thanks ever so" as you take his place. By the time he's realised what happened, you'll be away with your boozy booty. That said, should a sweaty, broad-shouldered young man sporting a tattoo of a swallow on his neck appear as competition for the spot in front, it is always wise to defer to his greater claim to the space.

Now let us allow our imaginations to wander: we have reached the bar...

Heroic single-mindedness or luck has secured us an uncomfortable position at the front, sandwiched so tightly we can't tell our neighbour's arse from his elbow. Now, how do we get our drinks? Natural justice might posit that, having patiently endured the strains of the pub throng, the doughty punter will find a smiling barman as soon as he reaches the front. Natural justice is not, unfortunately, a concept that has ever sat well with the English.

The key task now is to catch the barman's eye. This wasn't so difficult in the age of the career barman, but most modern bar staff are Australian. Years of squinting into the sun have rendered them blind to desperate punters. That, and their attitude of 'Couldn't give a dingo's testicle'. The temptation to shout or to wave money around in the air must be repressed - a control which is innate in the English. Rather, the careful employment of amateur psychology, subtle thespianism and outright bribery is required to guarantee success. The following three rules demonstrate this point:

1. A barman likes a confident punter who appears to have adequate reserves of cash. He hates arrogance, and he loves to refuse service. Draw your own conclusion.

2. An appearance of moderate, but not extreme, dehydration often clinches service. It is a barman's vocation to quench thirst, but it is also a barman's right to dismiss pathetic over-acting. A punter doing an impression of Ben Hur crossing the desert without food or water is guaranteed ignominious failure.

3. Although tipping in cash is not done (see below), convention allows a customer to buy the barman a drink. When the barman asks, "Anything else?" he means, "Buy me a drink and I'll serve you quicker next time round".

In summary: try to appear rich, thirsty, and benevolent, but avoid looking like Princess Margaret at a charity champagne do.

2. The traditional country pub

It must be noted that not all pubs are as busy as that. Some are busier. Fortunately, some enjoy quieter moments, so let us take a gentle ride to a traditional country pub in its somnolent post-prandial fug. In a corner ticks the antique mahogany grandfather clock. In another twitches the antique mahogany grandfather. The locals have returned to the fields, to wash down their five pints with a jug of scrumpy. Motes of dust haven't the energy to dance and farts hang in the air like zeppelins.

Three elderly gentlemen are at the bar musing over their last half inch of *Old Squirrel's Todger*. They are standing, partly in deference to their piles, and partly because that is what traditional old men traditionally do in any pub, no matter if there is a six deep throng waiting to be served. They are as purposeless and shiny as a horse brass, and twice as annoying. Sometimes it is hard to tell whether they are propping up the bar, or vice versa, but loneliness and latent alcoholism drive them to it. Its benefits: the companionship of other old men (beggars can't be choosers) and dim trouser stirrings every time the barmaid bends over. Given the English love of custom, habit and tradition, friendships formed at the bar continue unto death, and sometimes beyond - such is the tendency to let sleeping codgers lie.

Tossing off the remains of their *Todger*, laughing and farting heartily at Nobby's anecdote about his wartime action in the Pacific Rim, each geriatric is feeling giddy, relaxed and content, secure in the knowledge that their drinking session will stretch well into the wee hours that follow the Six o' Clock News.

When enters our pub novice.

The three wrinkled specimens notice his entrance immediately - using their sixth sense for strangers, and the loud clanging from the bed pan hanging above the door. Rubbing his head, our novice advances into the unknown. Rubbing their chins, the locals stare at the unknown. Itchy silence descends. The novice approaches the bar, coughs nervously, opens his mouth to order and...

PLUNK PLUNK PLUNK

Three glasses hit the bar loudly, three heads nod, three *Todgers* are replenished and three pub bores sit smugly in a bar presence that you can smell.

What to do (other than exact swift retribution with a three bore shotgun)?

Our novice should have approached the bar as confidently as mild concussion allows, grinned at the codgers and benevolently intoned, "After you, gents". Now three heads nod reluctantly, three upper sets grind a melancholy tattoo of defeat against three lower sets. Three eyes swivel jealously to see the barmaid's look of "I'll just see to these, then I'll be over to pull your *Todger* for you, Surrrr". Three glass eyes stay where they are, looking at a past when bloody townie foreigners stayed at home and you could discuss the war without fear of intruders from Europe.

Natural feudal deference, however, will ensue, trapping the novice in a corn circle of conversation. Invitations to the village fair (all three regularly enter their prize marrows), to down the yard of *Old Squirrel's Todger*, to sample the home-made chutney (only 62 per cent proof) and to hear about Nobby's adventures in the Pacific Rim soon have our novice so punch drunk that he offers to buy the next round. The pub bore is not as stupid as he looks.

Tipping

We now turn to an area of public life close to the heart of other nations, but absent from the English pub: tipping. In any English pub, the only acceptable tip is "Have a tenner on Chocolate Whipping Boy, in the 2.30, Haydock". "Haddock? Racing fish are they now? Whatever next?", and thus begins another interminable pub conversation.

The complete absence of the financial tip in the English pub is explained simply. Historically, punters were extremely poor. Some argue that the aristocracy's heavy taxation of peasants left them penniless. Others argue that the peasants were poor because they spent all their money in ale houses. Others still argue that they were peasants: being poor goes with the territory. Whichever, it is clear that hard-up peasants were not about to spend their hard-earned groats on the bar staff. So, since the Dark Ages, avoiding a tip has been as much a part of pub life as avoiding a round. Characteristically, both have survived intact into the more enlightened modern age.

Bitter

Bitter is the classic staple drink served in pubs. Or it was. It has now to compete with alcopops, spirits, lager and 'smoothflow' bitter - the chemical alternative.

So what is bitter, and why do the English drink it? Like England's other national drink (tea), bitter is brown, tastes like the very devil and is served just below boiling point all year round. Bitter brand names range from the generic: 'bitter', 'best', 'the usual', to the eccentric, our old friends *Strumpet's Fart* and *Old Squirrel's Todger*, revealing the twin English predilections for mediocrity and peculiarity. Bitter is an acquired taste, though few bother to acquire it now, preferring the chemical ease of lager. Yet they forget the main reason bitter became popular in the first place: it isn't gassy and doesn't bloat the stomach, so more of it can be drunk in a single session.

Bitter is served in measures of pints and half-pints - though the latter should never be countenanced: it's smaller, you see. Like bitter itself, the pint measure is unknown on the continent - possibly because of the metric system, possibly because Europeans are not as generous of spirit as the English when it comes to drinking. A warm, voluptuous drink is bitter, and it transports an Englishman to his favourite place: his mother's breast (though if he spills it down her frock she is not best pleased).

Biological resistance to bitter has been developed over centuries of English history. During the fifteenth century, traitors from the aristocracy were drowned in wine, but those from the peasantry were drowned in bitter, and were sometimes two days dead before they noticed. In addition, King Henry VIII forced would-be employees to drink ten pints of bitter in an hour as a test of their loyalty to the throne. Subjects who refused to drink, or those who wasted good beer by vomiting, were, naturally, beheaded - hence the phrase 'get it down your neck'. Like so many of Henry's appalling legacies (ginger beards, the Church of England, Greensleeves), bitter has remained an integral feature of English culture.

Drinking alcohol for pleasure and taste may not, on the face of it, seem to be an English convention. The French think they drink for pleasure. They are proud of the exquisite bouquets produced by their wines, cognacs and champagnes, but you can't get drunk on a smell alone. They appreciate the subtle distinctions in the flavour and 'body' of these various liquids, but they don't have an aftertaste - the beer swiller is still savouring his *Todger* two hours after supping it. The English bitter drinker does enjoy his pint - after all, let's save masochism for the bedroom. The French might have their cake and spend hours decorating it, but the Englishman eats the bloody thing. Generosity and quantity, plenty for all, and value for money. Liberalism and practicality captured in one drink. Hurrah!

Conclusion

If this chapter has proved anything, it is that the English enjoy drinking alcohol in public houses. It provides this most private of nations with a public forum, where the patient English can meet their fellows in neutral surroundings, away from the petty distractions of their lawns, gnomes and paving stones. The pub may be riddled with frustrating and absurd conventions, but to deny the English these would be to deny their identity. As many a punter has said, "I am what I drink and I am a bitter man".

Five: THE WEATHER
Fahrenheit 45.1

Of England's frailties and obsessions, the weather is the favourite on both counts. The country's climate is a constant source of bewilderment for a people unused to uncertainty and instability, yet the weather arrived on these islands first, so they should really know better. Sometimes, England basks in warm sunshine and its inhabitants suffer sunstroke. If an inch of snow falls, gritting lorries are despatched, causing major tailbacks on the roads. For the most part, though, the weather remains unsettled, not knowing which way to turn as the country is bombarded with cloud-bearing westerly winds from the Atlantic, occasional blasts from the Arctic and exceptional warm embraces from the Mediterranean.

This does not mean that England is not blessed with seasons: there are sometimes four in one year. In springtime, playful lambs briefly appear in the fields before they appear on the nation's dinner tables. In summer, people venture outdoors to huddle round barbecues for warmth. Autumn is hedgehog burning season and winter is called the festive season because it is grey and depressing.

Like so much else in England, however, the seasons often become confused. It is not unknown for January to bask in temperatures of 15 degrees Celsius, tempting fools to shed their clothes, or for June to shiver under a little Christmas snow. Summer heatwaves often arrive in the middle of October, realise they're late and promptly vanish.

Given this confusing situation, the English are left in a constant state of flux, not knowing whether to wear a thermal vest or a skimpy blouse, or if the drizzle will peter out after quarter of an hour or last all week.

The English are always surprised by the weather - which is, in itself, surprising. The English climate is, by nature, unsettled, but the English exhibit none of the weary acceptance one might expect from a nation that has been unceremoniously dumped on for at least the past couple of decades. Rather, they remain genuinely bemused by the twists and turns of the climate, the potential course of which is a source of national debate for all. This is called 'wondering what it's going to do'.

Let us examine the meteorological rationale for the English climate.

England is situated approximately three thousand miles across the Atlantic from North America and, being an island, sits in the middle of the sea. The prevailing wind in our world blows from west to east, known by meteorologists as 'westerly'. This means that the wind has travelled over three thousand miles of sea, whipping moisture up into cloud, before it arrives over the west of England and dumps its load. However, the gulf stream carries its warmth to the west coast, too, so at least the sea is slightly tepid in summer. The clouds have dribbled all over England before they reach the east coast, so this side of the country is drier. Unfortunately, it faces the North Sea, which is freezing all year round.

To say that England only suffers with rain is like saying an aristocrat only enjoys sadism. In fact, he enjoys many forms of sexual humiliation and pain. So it is with the weather: observations that the English have no weather save for the constant threat of rain, rain itself, or a touch of brightness in between rain showers are simply untrue. The vagaries of high and low pressure - represented by the isobars running up and down the weatherman's map like a cat o' nine tails - dictate that predominant patterns are often turned on their head and other influences slip in by surprise. A flick of high pressure here may produce an arctic blast or a taste of the Sahara. A lick of low pressure there may bring sleet, hail or just a hint of drizzle. And usually all in one afternoon.

England is known as a temperate country. This means that, despite constant fluctuations in the weather, the climatic extremes to which the nation is exposed are not really *that* extreme. It may be cloudy one minute and sunny the next, but the population is unlikely to ever be affected by monsoon floods or dry season famines. It must seem strange, then, that the English hold the peculiarities of their climate in such high regard when many other parts are regularly destroyed by theirs. Is it insecurity or naivety that has the English at crisis point whenever the temperature takes a slight turn?

In winter, when the temperature dips below zero degrees Celsius, a national emergency ensues. Schools close as their heating systems break down, having been left on all summer. This ensures that children develop a keen personal interest in the weather from an early age. The rail network comes to a complete standstill as 'the wrong type' of snow falls. That the authorities have not yet imported the right sort is just another indictment of the state of England's weather defences. On the roads, a ballet of mayhem ensues, with cars gliding gracefully into each other on 'black ice' - a curious euphemism employed by motorists to divert attention from their bad driving. During these exceptional conditions, the weather forecasts attract record viewing figures, and the government issues official advice on how to cope - sometimes even offering emergency funds to old people so they can use two bars instead of one on their gas fires. For many this is not enough and they flood onto the streets where it is warmer. In bus queues, they chat incessantly to keep the circulation going.

Here we find a typical elderly member of the working-class planning to visit the town centre to buy some thick tights and thermal gloves. Ironically, had she stayed indoors, she would not have needed them, but this does not occur to her. Neither does the prospect of ending up in hospital with double pneumonia, the simple soul.

"It's bloody cold today, isn't it? Feels like your blood's freezing up. I saw Elsie Sykes slip over and the ambulance man said she'll probably need a new right hip. Poor sod's just nicely got over her hysterectomy."

Pause.

"I hear Old Bert's been taken to the Infirmary with suspected pleurisy and flu and it'll be a miracle if my bloody chilblains don't come back...Still that bloody winter of 1947 was worse. Now that's what I call a winter - not like these modern ones. People were dying all over the place. Uncle Fred - bless his heart - his dentures chattered so much, they snapped in half. He was eating a meat and potato pie at the time. Put him off for life. His favourite, too."

Pause.

"Aye, that was a year. Colder here than in Russia, our Harry said."

After an hour-and-a-half of winter-related anecdotes, our representative will come to the conclusion that the public transport system has broken down completely.

"Didn't really expect it to turn up, but you live in hope, don't you?"

One by one the people in the queue give up hope of getting to the office, factory or thermal section of Marks & Spencer. They carefully slide home to sit in front of the fire, a warming cup of tea in hand, to watch television reports of the catastrophic effect the snow is having on national life.

Conversely, when the temperature rises to the unaccustomed level of seventy degrees Fahrenheit, office air conditioning units burn out, having worked all winter keeping people cool. For one day in August it is fixed, and blasts freezing air into a room full of people in skimpy summer attire, before burning out once more. People fall asleep on one side while sunbathing, and arrive at work the next day looking like the Phantom of the Opera. Dehydration and sunstroke are rife, both caused by sitting for too long in beer gardens. Hosepipes and sprinklers are banned because of drought conditions, and everyone marvels that, with so much rain falling during the rest of the year, none of it hits the reservoirs. People vow to live in reservoirs come autumn, as they'll be the only dry places in the country. Old people stand in bus queues, in their winter macs. They talk incessantly to let hot air escape. We return to the same old woman, this time planning to buy some factor 30 sun lotion and a pair of unfashionable sunglasses. Ironically, had she stayed indoors, she would not have needed them, but this does not occur to her. Neither does the prospect of rocketing blood pressure and a massive heart attack, the simple soul.

"Christ, I'm hot. It's sweltering. I'm sweating like a pig. Jimmy Swales has just been treated for third degree burns at the Infirmary...Old, err...what's-her-name - Irene O'Flahertie's been rushed in with suspected sun-stroke. And if that unsightly heat rash round my privates doesn't come back, I'll be amazed."

Pause.

"Still, I remember July 1964 - the fifteenth it was - like it was yesterday. My old dad, bless his soul, came home from work looking as white as angel's wings. He'd sweated so much his face was plastered with salt. Eighty degrees it was that day - weatherman said so on the wireless. God bless my old pa. He sat in his favourite chair - the tartan one with the cigarette burns on the arms - and closed his eyes. 'I'll just have a nap,' he said...Died within an hour, still sweating. Mother always blamed the heat. Doctor blamed his Woodbines, bitter and fried bread."

Pause.

"I dunno. Makes you think...and if this blessed bus ever turns up it'll be a miracle," she concludes, as the rest of the queue start silently praying.

After another hour-and-a-half, the people in the queue, still a little disturbed by the old woman's recollections, start to drift away. With most of the bus company laid up in bed with cold flannels on their brows, the service has been abandoned for the day. They return to their homes, to lie in cold baths and listen to live radio reports of the heat-wave's sensational effects on national life.

Talking about the weather

The English relish any opportunity to talk about the eccentricities of their weather. This obsession can best be illustrated by an examination of the postcards the English send from their seaside resorts to loved ones - even relatives -

reassuring them that they have not drowned in the sea.

The first line on an Englishman's postcard provides a weather report, as do the next ten and he starts his message with:

'Weather much the same as at home.'

'Weather indifferent, but the sun shone for ten minutes while we were unpacking.'

'Too hot - am horribly sun burnt.'

'The weather's completely spoiling an otherwise mediocre holiday.'

Given the limited writing space on the back of a postcard, there is just enough room left to give a few lurid details of stomach bugs, before adding the recipient's address. Not a riveting read, English postcards - unless one learns how to read between the lines.

As a repressed people, the national obsession with what it's going to do provides the English with a useful emotional shorthand. Where others offer up a 'How are you?' as an opening gambit, the Englishman uses his, 'What do you think of the weather then?' - or some variation. On his postcards we have observed that the conventional 'Wish you were here' - which is veering on the emotionally liberated - can be substituted with 'Weather awful'. It means the same thing, but allows the tricky subject of emotion to be discussed in a code of weather. Hence such phrases as: 'It's looking a bit miserable', and, 'Hope it cheers up later', which are self explanatory. Others include:

'I think it's turning to rain' - a sure sign of latent alcoholism.

'It's murderous out there' - make your excuses and leave quickly.

'It's meant to brighten up later' - I'm on Prozac.

'Isn't it close?' - I'd like to discard my underpants forever.

These metaphors, of course, have limits for the emotionally wary English. They would not dream, for instance, of going as far as Buddy Holly with, 'It's raining in my heart'. 'Don't like the look of that sky much', is going quite far enough.

In this vein, someone claiming that, 'It's raining cats and dogs' may seem to have run mad. They have not. Ever an inventive race, the English keep their patience with good humour and imagination. To merely state, 'It's raining' is boring, and will have most English people making their excuses to leave the conversation. So metaphors and similes are employed, many of them involving animals.

The aforementioned 'cats and dogs' example dates from the Middle Ages. Primitive drainage systems were inadequate to the challenge literally thrown down by a cloudburst, causing an untimely end for the local strays. When the waters receded, revealing the dead bodies of cat and dog alike, the dim-witted peasantry thought the unfortunate creatures had fallen from the sky. Drainage problems could also be the origin of 'It's pissing down'.

'I wouldn't put a cat out on a night like this' expresses the dread most animal-lovers harbour to subjecting a cat to inclement weather. The fact that the stubborn feline would sooner scratch out its owner's eyes than be carried forcibly into a downpour is neither here nor there.

'It's cold enough to freeze the balls off a brass monkey' is believed by some to have a sea-faring root: a brass monkey being the frame in which cannon balls were stacked. This is highly unlikely, though, and most English people take the phrase to mean that the weather is cold enough to freeze the testicles off a brass monkey, which makes much more sense.

For the visitor, an understanding of these conversational openers can be invaluable. Beginning a conversation with a comment about the weather could lead to partial acceptance, even appreciation, by the host population. Given the enormous English appetite for meteorological fare, he who broaches the subject shows cultural awareness and assists in temporarily dispelling the widely-held English belief that foreigners are on no account to be trusted.

For example, a foreigner finds himself in a quiet public house, has managed to order some drinks and is wishing to engage a nearby barfly in conversation. Having checked for the absence of tattoos, and an overabundance of neck muscles, he should make a casual observation on the weather. Why not the classic opener: "Nice weather for this time of year"?

The barfly is startled from his state of morose self-pity, and will not only respond enthusiastically with his own comments about recent meteorological events, but will immediately take the foreigner to his heart. Following an extended weather-related dialogue based on the English climate, the barfly will then ask about the climatic conditions of the foreigner's native land. Cross-cultural interaction will be established, providing a rare opportunity for the English to discover that some foreigners really aren't that bad.

The weather forecast

Weather forecasters never get it right, but they are the only people who get to talk about the weather on national television, which is why they are watched obsessively ten times a day. The forecasters' faces are more familiar to the English than most Hollywood stars.

The Meteorological Office is the government body responsible for monitoring the English weather, and it rightly takes great pride in its groundbreaking research into what the weather might do. For years they predicted an onslaught of velcro clouds, but they never appeared. They have been replaced by computer graphics now, which are prettier but no more meaningful

Strangely, a large part of the weather forecast predicts what happened in the past. The presenters gladly provide essential historical and comparative statistics for the English population to use in their discussions. For example, during a sweltering period, the following sample text might be used by the presenter:

"If tomorrow reaches 70 degrees Fahrenheit - that's Gas Mark Seven in new money - this will officially have been the longest heat-wave since 1977, which was a record breaker, as I'm sure many of you remember. But we're nowhere near 1768, when several thousand people reportedly died from heat exhaustion, and the Thames dried up. Today, London was hotter than Beirut, which is admittedly having an unusually cool period. But let's put this all into perspective: Dubai was sweltering in temperatures of 120 degrees. Enjoy the nice weather while you can, though. An ugly-looking depression is steaming in from the Atlantic, as you can see from the satellite photograph. This promises a return to cooler and more changeable conditions for the weekend."

Following this, families around the country look at each other and ask, 'What did he say it was doing tomorrow?'

Essentially the English know to expect a little bit of everything, and stare at the forecast just to confirm this ambiguity.

Even more baffling than TV forecasts, but far more entertaining, is Radio Four's cult favourite: the Shipping Forecast, which purports to be a forecast for shipping, but is in fact five minutes of dreamy poetry. Magical names like Dogger, Biscay, Lundy Fastnet and North Utsira beguile the listener's ear. 'Malinhead, good' intones the announcer. And yes, it is good, though no-one knows what it means - which is why it's a joy to listen to. An other-worldly seascape removed from lows over Basingstoke, and immaterial to everyday life. Weather as escapism.

Conclusion

The ever-changing weather, then, is the inspiration behind most social chatter, providing those who talk about it best with with cult TV status. It also keeps umbrella manufacturers working over-time, thus contributing to national prosperity. But, for those with an aversion to a changeable climate, for those who do not enjoy discussing it at every available opportunity and for those who fail to see the innate beauty of an isobar map, England is most definitely not the place to be.

Six: The Queue

Get thee behind me, Satan

We have already visited two of the more familiar queues in English society, though the queue to be served at the bar is more accurately described as a scrum. The queue at the bus stop epitomises the more classic scenario, where the English wait patiently in line. Later in this chapter, we shall queue at the post office, the suburban shop and the more high profile and fashionable queues such as those for the Wimbledon tennis championships and the department store January sales.

The queue is considered to be typically English, but there are other nations to whom queuing is no strange business. The main difference is that most of these are former communist countries in the Eastern bloc, where queues are a matter of life and death and usually culminate in the purchase of a stale loaf or half a potato. So, it is not the act of queuing itself that is quintessentially English, but the peculiar motivation that pushes the English to do it at all. Our exploration of this leads us to the very core of the nation's psychology as we journey into the deepest suburban mentality.

The English ability to wait-and-see, to take things as they come, is perfectly suited to the queue. What could fit the patient English psyche better than standing in a line moving at the speed of a glacier? But for a deeper understanding of the queue's contribution to English society, we must also consider its social function: what positive role could it possibly play? Surely the English don't queue just to prove how patient they are (although this is a handy bonus). Why should this phenomenon, usually associated with tedium and personal strife, be seen in anything but a negative light at all? In this land of the absurd, the answers are not difficult to find.

Let us take our place in several different queues, but instead of staring at the floor, we'll glance around and see if we can't get to the bottom of this queuing business, if not just the bottom of the person in front.

The Post Office Queue

This is one of the most enduring and heavily populated forms of queue, especially towards the end of the month, when people renewing their car tax swell the ranks of pensioners, benefit claimers and giro cashers.

Many post offices are hangovers from a time when the English took pride in public buildings, boasting grand, expansive and beautifully tiled old halls. These vistas of public space make the ideal location for a queue, allowing it to grow, twist, turn and spiral, mostly under one roof. It certainly resembles the foreign queues beamed to the English in their living rooms: 'A mass of humanity on the move', as refugees from the high street shuffle interminably forward. A great line of clerks' counters stretches the entire length of the building, and somewhere near the end of the hall, a dim light signifies that one of them is open for business. A fug of silence hangs in the air, broken only by wailing babies, toddlers running amok, old women nattering to no-one in particular, and the coughs and sneezes of a drizzle-soaked populace.

As we stand in the post office queue, what do we notice first? That we've been queuing out on the pavement for a quarter of an hour already. Yes, what else? Someone's dog is eyeing our brogues with a nasty glint in its eye. Very possibly. But mainly that the post office queue is populated by a broad cross-section of the English: the working and the unemployed, the rich and the poor, the young and the old. It's another of England's contradictions - hanging onto a segregating class system, but giving everyone a form that must at some stage be taken to the post office. Bureaucracy - the great leveller.

The post office has always offered an impressively eclectic range of products: stamps, car tax certificates, television licences, social security payments and gas tokens, for instance. It also provides an impressively eccentric level of customer service - ensuring that whatever the time of day, a significant queue develops. Given the post office's heroic attempt to service the needs of the nation's drivers, television watchers, gas users and underclass (amongst others), the harassed counter clerks spend their days in a state of constant confusion and despair, often giving pension payments to young single mothers or gas tokens to those on electric.

For the rare visitor who simply wishes to buy a stamp for her postcard, the effect of these apparently irrelevant activities can stick in the throat, especially if she's still fuming when she licks it.

The one counter clerk at position twelve has just provided yet another of his unlimited range of services. The queue shuffles forward. It moves again. So soon? Ah, the faulty bulb above position four has just claimed another victim - the position is not open. Back to the end of the queue, because the next-in-line is jealously guarding his now exalted position. Right, the customer at twelve has finished changing nationality, here we go. Striding smugly forward, next-in-line is halfway to the counter when a sign appears saying 'Position Closed'. Position six has opened instead, but the old woman behind him is already there, and no-one is letting him back in. The wheel of fate spins once more to dish out its injustice.

In the midst of it all, the visitor is still waiting to buy a stamp for her postcard. She must weather the storm of adversity. The English have to.

To gain a full understanding of the English psyche the post

office queue is without compare. It should be an essential part of the curious observer's itinerary - however irritating the experience proves. What have we discovered so far? A mix of untold patience, harsh convention, hostile self-service and stoicism in the face of fate. There is a feeling that everyone is in this together, but this is prevented from developing into genuine camaraderie by mass paranoia: everyone is out to steal your place. The tension provided by this contradiction of friendliness tempered by suspicion is the glue that holds the queue together. By unspoken mutual consent, it is agreed that the queue is the only way to prevent death and mayhem - fatalism is better then fatality - and as any pensioner will tell you, a pension is just not worth dying for.

Unfortunately, although the queue prevents social upheaval, it also tends to prevent conversation. This rule does not extend to domestic pets, though, for a dog will be patted, stroked and praised by at least eighty per cent of those in the queue. The owner meanwhile is universally ignored. Dogs are innocents, at least as far as queuing is concerned. If a dog jumps the queue he is unlikely to be served, because dog licences have long since been abolished.

Most English people will speak if spoken to, but will not start conversations. There are two notable exceptions: the mad and the elderly. The former know no better. The latter are desperate to say everything they have bottled up in former queues, before they die. The young and the middle-aged accept this convention with equanimity, realising that one day the time will come for them to bombard the post office with their own ranting.

The typical spokesperson is an old woman, not afraid to bandy legs or bandy words. She has tightly-permed hair, dyed violet or blue, and has 'seen it all before'. She is expected to analyse a defined range of subjects during an extended monologue, and her delivery is interjected by embarrassed nods, occasional shuffling of feet and grating of teeth by the other members of the queue. Luckily for them, the merciful vagaries of the queue barriers mean that more than one of their number will bear the brunt of her rant.

First on her agenda are 'the youth of today.'

"Kids! - no bloody respect these days - in my day we had respect - beaten into us it was - if you cheeked someone off in the street you got a clip round the ear - ought to be more of that now - adults beating up children in public - does 'em good - hooligans they are now - cracked out of their heads on whizz cigarettes - vandals and joy riders the lot of 'em - bring back the birch - hang the lot of 'em, I say -'part from my grandkids that is."

Pause.

"Bloody kids...having this sex they are at fourteen - I was married at fourteen and had three kids but I didn't have sex 'till I was twenty-five - and these bloody single mothers - what! - no such thing in my day - we were all war widows - I blame the pill - no more headaches you see - and they're at it like knives - disgusting that's what it is - off with different ones every night - in my day you wed and you stayed wed - my husband beat that into me all right - idle shiftless good for nothing - like some of these now..."

It will be noted from this extract that the spokesperson would not be a welcome guest at a dinner party for the chattering classes.

She continues.

"Never heard of beggars in my day - scrounging around without a shred of decency and self-respect - should clean themselves up - have a shave and get out to work - like I did for forty years - idle good-for-nothings must like it - parents should have given 'em a kick up the backside - that would of kept them at home - didn't do my son any harm - (mind you, haven't seen him for fifteen years) - they don't know hardship these homeless

- don't know what it's all about - I've worked my fingers to the bone - I've had a miserable life - why should they be happy, I ask you…"

Pause.

"I suppose it's not their fault though…"

A glimpse of human feeling?

"…it's these darkies taking their jobs - coming here in the Fifties just 'cos they was asked to - bloody disgrace - can't understand a word they say - 'cept that nice Mr Singh at the corner shop - but 'is kids! - think they're English just 'cos they was born here and speak it better'n I do - coming back from Oxbridge University with their airs and graces - lah di dah - I say if you can't speak English you shouldn't be here - it is bloody England when all's said and done - should be a language test at the airport - that'd do the trick - this isn't bloody Calcutta - can I lean on you love?- ta-"

Temporary relief is offered as she bends down to adjust her support tights.

Then, "Gaw that's better - bleedin' things been giving me gyp all day - I'm on a waiting list for me varicose veins but what good's that - bloody NHS is up the spout - 'scuse my French dear - government's spent it all on homeless people - live in luxury some of 'em - they take with one hand - and then take with the other - I'm not greedy - never have been - never been able to afford it for a start - but it's bloody disgusting - you'll learn when it's too bloody late - when you've lost your teeth and your water-works don't work right anymore - we fought a war for you, y'know?"

By this time, most of the queue are under the impression that she is the first wave of a new invasion, and stare at the floor hoping either that she or they will disappear into it.

Further down the queue, a second elderly lady is nattering away - to no-one in particular - with her reflections on the institution of the queue itself. We find this old campaigner relating snippets of her own extensive queuing history. Often she'll have several cronies in the crowd, regulars to whom she can turn for verification because they've been subjected to her favourite anecdotes on many previous occasions.

"Oo I don't mind queuing really - this one's nothing to what we endured in the war - do you remember Ethel?" (Ethel nods with resignation) "Waiting eight hours in the rain for a rasher of bacon and a bit of powdered egg ...and I didn't even like powdered egg - AAAAaaaaahahahahaah!"

She nearly chokes on her hysterical laughter.

"Those were the days though - it was nice really - not like nowadays, everybody so miserable - Oh the songs people were always singing songs - we'd have a lovely singsong to keep our spirits up what was my favourite now..." (At this point, there is a very real danger that she will break into song, using the tremulous, warbling technique favoured before 1920.) "We'll meet again don't know where...how did it go, Ethel?" (Having completed her act, she spends a little time regaining her composure and readjusting her gusset before continuing her reminiscence.)

"Dunkirk spirit that's what it was - oo there's Mr Swales - wasn't it Mr Swales? - Dunkirk spirit? - everyone in the same boat - well not at Dunkirk they weren't, that would have been a squash - oh what am I saying? AAAAaaaaahahahahaah! - I remember once - 1943 it was - March - a bright spring day - me and my husband long since gathered were queuing at the fish shop waiting for some fish - we'd heard they got some fish in you see - well who should come and see us but the Queen Mum, Gaw blesser, though she was just the Queen then, as if she didn't have enough on her plate! - come right up to us she did and said - what are you queuing for? - well I just blushed, couldn't speak, but my husband long since gathered said to her he said - fish Ma'am - just like that - oh he had a way with words - how we laughed - fish Ma'am, just like that and it was a fish shop you see? AAAAaaaaahahahahaah!"

By this stage, most of the queue are gnawing their fists in agony, but this is preferable to telling her to shut up. Unthinkable? No, very thinkable, just undo-able.

The post office queue, then, offers enforced fair play at the cost of considerable masochism - thus perfectly suiting the English psyche. The English like to feel that they are having to 'put up with things', indeed they are martyrs to this cause and the post office queue offers a range of patience-testers unequalled anywhere else in the country

The shop queue

The shop queue has altered in form over the last twenty years, as supermarkets have replaced smaller shops. Instead of queuing in several small queues at several small shops, the English now experience just the one big queue in the one big shop. The supermarkets do offer at least fifteen big queues to choose from, but, in keeping with modern consumer trends, they are all exactly the same. However, the queuing dynamic has hardly changed, despite variations in the form.

Most English shop queues boast such an impressive number of elderly people that the hierarchical convention attached to the post office queue proves unworkable. Here, the aged simply talk to the person next in line, while simultaneously eavesdropping on all the conversations around them. This allows for both rewarding conversation and the collection of vital gossip. Here, therefore, we find the true apogee of the English queue - with its potential fully realised.

Historically, England's shopkeepers understood the following timeless truth: if English people saw a queue outside a shop, they could not resist joining it. Innate conformity and a fear of missing out dictated that the Englishman would find himself standing in line, while the shopkeeper kept the queue artificially bloated by chatting for too long with each customer he served. If the queue failed to move with sufficient dispatch, however, the man at the back would be faced with a choice. He could remain static until the shopkeepers' conversation had ended, then shuffle a few inches closer to the front. Or he could leave the queue and find somewhere else to shop. Leaving a queue goes against the English grain, so the shopkeeper could depend on the vast majority of its members to stay exactly where they were.

The English hate change - which is why old women always pay with it - and so the queue always persists. Supermarkets are too big to induce queues which spill onto the pavement, though the one at the 'express' checkout for ten items or less often comes close to it. It is here that we find the modern day equivalent of the shop queue of old. Express queues boast an impressive number of elderly people, all buying cat food and gossiping, eavesdropping, keeping an eye on the number of items in the baskets of newcomers, watching the young mother's baby shoplift chewing gum, hoping the alarms will go off when she leaves the shop. Elsewhere cash back services and faulty PDQ machines ensure that no-one in the supermarket leaves without a wait.

The bus queue

We now return to the bus queue we joined in the previous chapter (having lost our place, of course, we rejoin it at the end). This specimen is not defined by barriers, or the linear form of the supermarket queue, and is therefore the most fragile. Still, it provides the English with an ideal place to allow full rein to their twin addictions - order and hierarchy. The anchor for the bus queue is the bus stop itself. From this pole extends our ragged mass of humanity once more, except they are no longer on the move. A bus queue is a sporadic thing, growing quickly, then being decimated in one go when the bus arrives and runs it over.

As more people arrive the queue starts to resemble that famous painting, *Bus Stop,* by Hieronymous Bosch, descending into what appears to the untrained eye to be nothing short of anarchy. Indeed, it often resembles a randomly positioned group of people, rather than the ordered line one might expect. The elderly form the head of the queue, because they arrive half an hour before the bus is due. Behind them, in order, come various commuters, students, school children, the unemployed and the drunk who always stands next to you. It is the duty of the elderly to complain and gossip loudly about how anti-social the rest of the queue is. Everyone else should defer to the elderly, even when they're elbowing their way to the front, swinging their walking frames into your shins. Commuters will stand quietly in their Macintoshes, as will students in their assorted woollenry. As for the school children... there is a special breed of school child bred to cause havoc in bus queues. Reason dictates that pleasant children do exist, but why they never catch buses remains a mystery to science. A cacophony of inept flirting, fart noises, thrown fists and thrown lunch boxes emanates from these juvenile cretins. The drunk just mumbles and smells until he spots you, at which point his eyes light up and he ambles over offering bonhomie and special brew. You wonder what it is that he knows about you, that makes you viable as a soul mate.

Each member has an exact knowledge of his or her place in this queue. The hierarchy of arrivals is consistently calculated and everyone knows when they arrived. This is important because the bus could stop at any point along the length of the queue. Should the gaggle of pensioners at the front be standing ten feet from the bus, and a solitary postal worker be standing at its doors, the postman will wait for them to board, as long as the chronology of arrivals dictates this to be the appropriate action.

Queue convention dictates that each person after him will follow in exact order until the bus is ready to move to the next stop where the pantomime is staged again.

This is all ammunition ready for the dread occurrence: a queue jumper. The queue jumper is a dastardly and unsporting individual - a pariah, a hyena, an opportunistic cad. Several are the ploys he may take to gain his sorry end, and all are underhand. The sneakiest is to loiter near the front. Obvious you may say, but the aim is to look as if he's not part of the queue, has no interest in the queue, couldn't care less if the queue lived or died. When the bus arrives, he simply ambles onto it, as if it is his natural right, or as if carried along with the flow - a more cunning move. A bolder ploy, almost to be admired for its audacity, is to exploit the neutrality of the bus stop pole itself. Just because a bunch of near-sighted old folk have chosen to stand on one side of it, doesn't mean that the other side is not for queuing too. If the jumper can pull this off with authority, a legitimate queue may actually form behind him, confounding everything. Or, more traditionally, he can just push in.

Not to worry, though, the queue will always spot him, and with fair play and justice uppermost in their minds, they will unleash a battery of muttering, ominous shifting and pointed looks. The queue is so adept at this they can keep it up while the jumper boards, while he pays, during the journey and even as he walks past the window having disembarked. Then they sit back with a look of 'that'll teach him'.

Perhaps the thing to remember is that most career queue jumpers are English too. A polite, "Excuse me, the back of the queue is down there", will elicit an equally polite, and equally unconvincing, "So sorry, didn't realise", and off he'll toddle. If the swine says, "So?", then he is undoubtedly a foreigner and beyond hope.

Famous queues

Certain queues have become notorious national institutions. Indeed, some members of these famous queues join them for their intrinsic merits as queues, rather than their original purpose.

The Wimbledon ticket queue. A national sporting event televised yearly, unless it's sunny, in which case tennis is shown instead. Some members of this queue almost break down from the joy of belonging to it. Others simply stare into the cameras, unsure of where they are, but happy nonetheless to have joined such a famous queue.

The queue for department store January sales. Those who initiate these are lauded as national celebrities over the Festive Season and are constantly interviewed by TV reporters from their sleeping bags. They proudly boast of the fifty hours they have spent lying on the pavement (and the £1.30 they made from passers-by who thought they were homeless). Then they get trampled to death rolling up their groundsheet when the doors open.

The queue for 'the Ladies'. One cubicle and much ado with underwear and laying paper on the seat equals a vast and bad tempered line of women.

The queue for 'the Gents'. No, no. They're not queuing for the Gents, just waiting for their wives to finish in the Ladies.

Conclusion

In the words of our foreign correspondent: "The scene here is a mass of humanity on the move... except they're not moving. Here we have the lonely, the dispossessed, and those just popping down the shops. Where they come from, nobody knows, wherever they're going, they're going to be a long time getting there. Why they do it is uncertain, but they seem to like it. They are looking at me with bewilderment. Some are tutting. Others still, are being run over by a bus. An old woman approaches proffering haemorrhoid cream. I think it is high time I made my excuses and left..."

Seven: ENGLISH DIALECTS
Bad Language?

As one might expect, most people in England speak English. Unfortunately, the majority speak with such pronounced regional accents it is often hard to believe their language is English at all. The operatic Liverpool Scouser is misunderstood by the Scandinavian-influenced Geordie from Newcastle – and vice-versa. The chirpy Cockney's rhyming slang is a million linguistic miles from the bunged up whine of the Brummie from Birmingham. To the untrained ear, the West Country drawl and the ferocious Yorkshire dialect certainly sound like languages – but they are surely not English.

The continuing popularity of these accents proves to be an inconvenience not only for the English themselves, but also for visitors. If the English cannot understand each other, what chance does a foreigner have? The helpful upshot of our discussion shows visitors will find communication with the natives virtually impossible.

We start, however, with the variation of the language that most of the English should aspire to, if not understand. It has long served as the ideal or standard which most fail to match: the Queen's English.

The Queen's English

The Queen sets a perfect example in many behavioural spheres: her expertise in the realm of the stiff upper lip is legendary, for example, but speaking through it does give her rather a strange accent.

From very early in life, the Queen and the other members of her noble class are taught to value tradition and continuity above all else, which puts a necessary emphasis on in-breeding. After all, if one is considered to be of a pre-eminent calibre, finding someone with whom to mate becomes rather limited. One usually has to look to the monarchies of other nations. As a result, England's monarchs have rarely been English. Thus they were able to learn the correct way to pronounce each word without the need to unlearn the vulgarities of every day English speech, though their own foreign vulgarities inevitably modified the end result. Historically, there was no need for monarchs to be understood by their subjects. They would hardly exchange pleasantries with the peasantry, so most of them spoke French, while the peasants spoke gutter-snipe. Now there is more of a need to be understood by the populace at large. Even so, the present Queen hardly appears to relish the mother tongue, which is why she sounds like a constipated child refusing to take a mouthful of food.

For those who have never been to the launch of a ship, or the opening of a hospital wing, the Queen's Christmas Day speech provides the ideal introduction to the Queen's speech. How does one follow too much stuffed turkey? Watching Her Majesty might not seem ideal, but it takes the mind off indigestion. Wearing a sensible dress and understated earrings, the Queen holds forth for ten minutes on the year that has passed and her country's official hopes for the year to come. There is another Queen's Speech at the annual opening of parliament in the autumn, but virtually no-one listens to this because it is all about politics.

A popularly-held belief is that the Queen talks 'with a plum in her mouth', but this seems wide of the mark. Certainly, she has never been known to spit masticated fruit over her listener. A more helpful description of her delivery is to imagine how one might speak while sitting on someone's finger. This helps us to explain the moderately shrill, slightly pained manner of her speech. Discomfort is evident in every syllable, and the unnatural, stilted delivery reflects slight distaste, just as if there was a large and unwelcome digit up the royal backside. When she has forced out the final words of her speech (traditionally "Is *Eastenders* on yet?"), the entire nation sighs with relief.

The results of the nation's attempts to emulate the Queen's mode of speech are mixed. The aristocracy has perfected the method. The upper-middle and chattering classes have developed their own variation on the sound, namely, talking through their arse. The rest of the middle class attempt to emulate the Queen's English - with varying degrees of failure. Meanwhile, the working and underclass do not even try to 'talk posh'.

The delivery of legitimate Queen's English is deliberate in the extreme - the lower orders' habit of dropping some aitches from their vocabulary, and picking up others that nobody wants, is rightly deplored by the nobility. Regional accents are also anathema to the aristocrat's sensitive ears. Textbook syntax is the foundation upon which aristocratic conversation proudly stands, even if it is cracked.

The Prince of Wales is perhaps the most well-known exponent of what might be termed 'the faltering method'. A constipated anguish accompanies even the most innocuous of statements: as we have seen, he usually acknowledges his mother with an "er" before each phrase. A further preoccupation with his large ears means that even short sentences are extended well beyond the reasonable. Here we can hear how Charles might sound of a morning (rendered phonetically).

"Would His Highness like one round of eggy soldiers this morning, or two?" asks his servant.

"Er, ears, ah... um. Ears eh thenk... mmm. Ah lits ear. Um ah, hum. Eh thenk, ears, eh thenk eh shell sur-face with... ears! Taste! Jest one rind." replies HRH.

"One round of toast. Very good, Sir."

This extended delivery means that the aristocracy rarely manages to say very much, but this perfectly fits the aristocratic disinclination to share emotions and thoughts. And despite this verbal handicap, the aristocracy is treated with the utmost respect by the other classes in English society. When an aristocrat opens his mouth, his social standing is immediately apparent: what little he says may be trivial, but the important point is *how* he says almost nothing. The aristocrat's Queen's English is sufficient for him to be accepted as superior by those who cannot speak it themselves - despite his inability to use it in any constructive manner whatsoever. Anyone else trying to imitate it will inevitably fail: the correct learning method is centuries of privilege and a breeding with foreign nobility. This is why received pronunciation was developed as an alternative.

Received Pronunciation

The English spoken by the upper-middle class and the chattering classes is known as Received Pronunciation, or Standard English. As we have seen, the Queen's English is a class-based tongue and the speaker gives nothing away about his geographical origins, in contrast to the lower orders who can be placed after their first unintelligible grunt. Like the nobility, speakers of Standard English aim to give no linguistic clues as to their regional background. But, given the slightly more relaxed delivery and the ability to get to the point, it is quite clear they do not hail from the aristocracy.

Standard English was developed by those without the benefit of the aristocrat's innate breeding, but who were nonetheless disgusted by regional accents - snobs, basically. Second generation *nouveau riche,* embarrassed because their working class roots were showing and they wanted to be taken seriously by those higher up the social scale. They just wanted to attend society dinners and gentlemen's clubs without being laughed at over the entrée. Meanwhile, with the advent of mass communication, the BBC wireless broadcaster needed to be understood by everyone and achieve the air of gravitas necessary to patronise an entire nation at once. (It is only in recent years that television presenters have learnt how to patronise in Scottish, Irish and Welsh accents too.) For these reasons, Standard English has evolved to its current, perfected state.

Its rules are significantly simpler than for Queen's English and are perhaps best described in negative terms. If the listener is able to place the speaker regionally, then the speaker is not speaking 'correctly'. The camouflaging of any regional accent is paramount, resulting in a bland but comprehensible adhesion to set pronunciation. Standard fluency brings considerable rewards

– flourishing careers, useful contacts with the upper crust and the grudging respect of those stuck with regional accents. No wonder so many millions spend their time patiently learning proper English.

Skilled exponents of Standard English always have a rationale for using their variant of the language - family advantage, financial gain or career advancement. But these factors are always dressed up as 'good breeding'. For those without pedigree or directed ambition, the intricacies of proper English always prove to be a major stumbling block. Without understanding why they want to speak properly - save for a vague desire not to appear 'common' - the vast bulk of the middle class embarrasses itself whenever it opens its mouth. The English suburbs burst with petty snobbery and rivalry, and where the spoken word is concerned, 'keeping up with the Joneses' is not good enough: one must be better than the Joneses at all costs. Let us investigate the results.

Our example follows a conversation between Mrs Smyth (pronounced 'Smythe') and her son's Oxford-educated school teacher, Mr Knox. Knox is a typical representative of the chattering classes: highly intelligent, articulate and capable, he has nonetheless foregone the material wealth offered by law or accountancy in order to spout his progressive opinions to children, wear a corduroy jacket with elbow patches and grow an unruly beard.

"Mrs Smith, how nice to see you, please sit down."

"It's Smythe, actually."

"Oh, I see."

There is an uncomfortable silence, as Mrs Smyth purses her lips dramatically, and Mr Knox allows himself a brief smirk.

"Now, young Giles has been having some difficulty with his grammar this term."

"Oh, I see. He has been somewhat, how can one say this

without sounding *de rigeur*...One has been having our problems with him. We've tried our best to bring him up properly, Gawd knows. But I don't know where he gets his language, his tongue. That boy next door, I shouldn't wonder. They shouldn't of let that family move in - spends all 'is time with 'im... Him. Ahem."

Mr Knox plays with his liberal beard until Mrs Smyth has finished. Regaining her composure, Mrs Smyth daintily clears her throat and changes tack.

"As I think the Bard himself said: 'The roots of education are sour, but fruit is sweet.'"

"That was Aristotle."

"What was?"

"The quote. 'The roots of education are bitter, but the fruit is sweet.'"

Mrs Smyth's expression darkens and she casts Knox a resentful glance. She then gets up and totters haughtily towards the science teacher for a further helping of humiliation.

Clearly, Knox is a new teacher. His life has been spent solely in the higher reaches of the middle class. He therefore has a great deal to learn about the culture of those in its middle and lower reaches, whose members try so hard to sound cultured. Their inevitable failure, however, does not cause any abandonment of their efforts. Quite the opposite. On future occasions, Mrs Smyth will simply endeavour to talk with even more cultivation and make a greater fool of herself, causing her listener hilarity and horror in equal measure.

So much for the higher levels of the linguistic spectrum, and its absurd imitations. We can now devote ourselves to some of England's regional accents. The Queen's and Standard English are strange, though comprehensible, variations of the language. The regional accents are just strange. Very, very strange.

Cockney

Let us begin in London, the home of the Cockney. A Cockney is traditionally a Londoner born within earshot of Bow Bells - the bells of St. Mary-le-Bow Church in the City of London - though this distinction is rarely maintained today. Anyone perceived to have a lower-class London accent is therefore likely to be labelled a Cockney, though they are most probably speaking 'estuary English', a nasal twang that originated around the Thames estuary in Essex, but which is now heard all over the south-east of England.

In both Cockney and estuary English, the proponent speaks rapidly, desperately filling each sentence with a multitude of unfinished words, in complete contrast to the aristocrat. The speed is attributed to the pace of London life and the Cockney's love of fast living, flash cars, designer clothes and shady deals. The phrase: 'How are you doing? Are you all right?' is translated into Cockney thus: 'Are doin'? Y'awight?'

The truly distinguishing feature of Cockney, however, is its use of 'rhyming slang'. When we consider that his delivery is already unintelligible, it seems hard to understand why the Cockney should wish further to encode his speech. But the English like codes and secrets and Cockney is simply an example of this. The Cockney may talk drivel, but at least he talks it in an amusing and inventive way.

Let's take a simple word like 'stairs'. In rhyming slang this becomes 'apples and pears'. So far, so good. However, the practised and experienced Cockney will often drop the second half of the phrase (the part which rhymes) and simply use the first word, which does not rhyme at all. He might say, 'I'm going to climb the apples', but he is still, in fact, planning to go upstairs. A similarly common abbreviation is 'syrup', short for 'syrup of figs' - wig. The experienced and ironic rhymer will seem not to have rhymed at all, but the implicit, unspoken part of the phrase does in fact rhyme ('fig' and 'wig').

A further complication arises when the first part of the phrase is so over-used that a rhyme for *it* gets invented. To illustrate our example, let's talk 'arse'. The original rhyme for arse was 'bottle and glass'. Perhaps this caused embarrassment in pubs and bars, with people asking to drink 'straight from the bottle' or men in fights 'losing their bottle'. For whatever reason, the word 'Aristotle' became popular as a substitute for 'bottle'. Of course, no self respecting Cockney is going to go about the place using a word of four syllables and so the abbreviation 'Aris' took its place. The astute will notice that 'Aris' sounds remarkably similar to 'arse', and may wonder why the Cockney bothered in the first place. Still, it can be claustrophobic living in the city: it's always nice to take the scenic route. And, by ensuring he is misunderstood by foreign and English tourist alike, he is able to rip them off to his heart's content.

The visitor to the capital is therefore well advised to study Cockney. The following is an admittedly short list – and the keen observer ought to buy a dictionary of the full complement of rhymes and implicit rhymes.

Plates = Plates of Meat = Feet
Frog & Toad = Road
Ice Cream Freezer = Geezer = Bloke = Man
Lady = Lady Godiva = Fiver = Five Pound Note
Ayrton = Ayrton Senna (the now deceased Brazilian Formula One racing driver) = Tenner = Ten Pound Note
Barnet = Barnet Fair = Hair
China = China Plate = Mate

Brummie

We now move northwards to the West Midlands, home of the Brummie - a bastardisation of the name of the area's largest city,

Birmingham. Despite certain economic pretensions, the city remains in London's wealthy shadow. The linguistic result is that the Brummie always seems to be whining in a peculiar sing-song - like back-to-front Welsh. Meanwhile, the Brummie's bunged-up nose, exacerbating this whine, is attributed to the iron-smelting industry, because the noxious fumes permanently block his nasal passages.

It is not at all uncommon for the listener, engaged in conversation with a representative from the Midlands, to drop off into a sound sleep, given the soporific effects of the accent. No-one has (as yet) cashed in on the enormous potential of the Brummie dialect as a cure for insomnia or, if they have tried, they didn't stay awake long enough to report back.

This is not to say that Brummies are boring. They may be insightful and witty conversationalists for all anyone knows, with an endless supply of inspiring anecdotes relating to iron-smelting, bridge-building and car-making. If one of them ever takes elocution lessons, perhaps we'll find out.

Returning to the phonetic method, we can have a listen to the Brummie's idiosyncratic approach to English. Let us take a thirsty Brummie, reasonably enough entering a café to ask for a cup of tea. In English this would read: "I'd like a cup of tea, please." In Brummie, the counter assistant would hear the following sounds: "Oid loyk a cop a tay, plays." He never gets it, of course, the assistant having dozed off almost immediately.

Scouse

Our English journey takes us further north, to the city of Liverpool. Here, the Scouser doesn't merely talk in sing-song, he is almost operatic. The tuneful and enthusiastic delivery of Scouse - based on the Irish jigs of the city's immigrant population - fits with the optimistic and humorous nature of its people. Scousers are thought to tell funny jokes about unemployment, petty crime and dodgy haircuts (their city's chief characteristics), though it is virtually impossible to understand them, without previous schooling in Scouse. This is a prospect so irritating, most people prefer to accept the Scouser's claim that he's a barrel of laughs.

The Scouser is named after an eighteenth century word, 'Lobscouse', a sailor's dish of stewed meat, vegetables and ship's biscuits. This delicacy evokes a time when the city of Liverpool was still a major national port. In the twentieth century, however, it has become synonymous with economic decline as few Scousers now work anywhere, let alone on ships.

Despite the present lack of maritime activity, centuries of shouting through high winds and salty sea spray have had a permanent effect on the accent. The Scouser therefore delivers his discourse with a plethora of rasping, throaty 'kh' sounds. The word 'like', which appears at least three times per Scouse sentence, is thus pronounced 'likkkkkkkkkkkhhhhe'.

The Scouser repeats his hackneyed phrases over and over again, so if the reader can imagine someone vigorously applying a cheese grater to Placido Domingo, then he may have an idea of how authentic Scouse sounds. Little wonder the Scouser is a laughing stock among his fellow countrymen.

Yorkshire

We now traverse the Pennines (a set of brooding hills covered with brooding sheep) and pitch our tent in Yorkshire. Here Emily Brontë based her famous 1847 novel, *Wuthering Heights*, detailing the doomed and impossible love of Cathy and Heathcliff. The reader is offered a snippet of the Yorkshire dialect according to Miss Brontë's original book which employed the phonetic method itself.

"'Aw sud more likker look for th' horse," he replied. "It 'ud be tuh more sense. Bud, aw can look for norther horse, nur man uf a neeght loike this as black as t'chimbley! und Hathecliff's noan t'chap tuh coom ut maw whistle - happen he'll be less hard uh hearing wi' ye!'"

The present author writes as a Yorkshireman, living ten miles from the setting of *Wuthering Heights*. Having read and re-read the passage, these are my thoughts. Heathcliff is mentioned. So are: a horse, something black and a whistle.

A stranger to this part of England might therefore reasonably expect to understand literally nothing. The contemporary lower orders of west Yorkshire are no longer chronicled by Miss Brontë, if only because she is dead, but their dialect is as ferociously ugly as it was during her short life. Yorkshire people claim they are hard-working, friendly folk with an ability to 'say what they mean and mean what they say'. A hollow boast when a translator is required for even the simplest of phrases.

Geordie

Our penultimate port of call takes us to the intemperate north-east - home of the Geordie. Famed for his love of football, meat pies and bottled brown ale, the Geordie provides conclusive proof that elocution lessons really ought to be part of the school curriculum.

The north-east is the closest part of the country to Scandinavia, whose inhabitants appear to communicate via the popular mumble, 'Hurt-de-gurt-de-gurt'. Indeed, the linguistic influence of the Nordic countries on the Geordie has been profound. Simply replace the furs with a Newcastle United Football Club shirt, and the seal club with a bottle of Newcastle Brown Ale and, voila: a fully-seasoned mumbling, inarticulate Geordie.

The Viking influence is illustrated in his favourite phrase, 'Howay the lads' - the very chant that Viking invaders used to scream as they raped and pillaged their way across the north-east. Although in Norwegian it means, 'Suffer, English scum!', the Geordie now reserves the catchphrase for when the football team scores or he finishes a bottle of brown.

Modern-day Scandinavians have rejected their barbaric past, and have embraced the civilising influences of furniture and education. As part of their quest for knowledge, Scandinavians have constructed an enviable understanding of the English language. In an ironic twist of fate, Geordies are famed for their careful dismantling of it.

West Country

As our journey comes to a close, it is perhaps only appropriate that we finally put our feet up in the West Country – that part of England known for its relaxed, unhurried way of life. The accent employed here is perhaps best not described as an accent at all, but rather as an extension of the resident's slow-paced, rural existence. The yokel's attitude of calm and contentment is evident in the way he idles his days away in the fields, drinking scrumpy straight from the apple press. Scrumpy is a noxious and highly intoxicating form of cider, even more vital to the yokel's sense of self than brown ale is to the Geordie.

The addling effects of this brew cause the West Country inhabitant to slur and drool over his simplistic vocabulary to the extent that it is often impossible to hear what he is saying above the hiccups, giggles and burps.

Rightly proud of his heritage, the West Country resident has been known to freely admit his dependence on cider. However, the phrase, 'I am a cider drinker' rarely emerges in such a clear fashion. Again, the phonetic method proves useful as a guide to the accent. In this case, one should aim not to snigger when the local bellows, 'Oayeeee arrrrm, oaaay zoidarrrr drraaankuur', simultaneously highlighting the effect of the region and the scrumpy on his accent.

Conversations in the West Country rarely venture beyond the subject of scrumpy, but they take so long that only visitors with endless reserves of patience, and exceptionally sturdy constitutions, would be advised to even attempt communication there.

Conclusion

The English language is alive and well, as evinced by its flourishing slang and colourful accents. The influences on it have always been strange and foreign, and long may they continue to be so - just as long as no-one can understand what the typical Englishman is saying.

Eight: FOOD

'The way to an Englishman's heart is through his belly, especially if you're on overtime.'

\- Heart surgeons' saying

Generations of the patient English have eaten all kinds of bland nonsenses served up before them and, as one would expect, they have never complained about their food. They have accepted its mediocrity with good grace, some even taking pride in the questionable culinary traditions handed down by previous generations. These customs include the over-cooking of vegetables, the frying of ...well, whatever happened to be near the pan at the time, the preparation of unadulterated cholesterol and the turning of mince into 'mince with carrots'. In this chapter, we assess a variety of English dishes in terms of taste, nutritional content and capacity to induce heart disease. Our conclusions are an inspiration to any foreigner planning to open a restaurant in England.

The most famous English cook, Delia Smith, recently wrote a best-selling book showing the English how to boil eggs and make toast. The English bought millions of copies and a few have now mastered the basic kitchen manoeuvres, like opening the fridge. In short, the English are not a nation of cooks. Unadventurous to the point of timidity, they would have continued to eat their fish and chips, Sunday Roast and Full English Breakfasts with heartless abandon, were it not for the recent influx of foreign foods and recipes.

The increasing popularity of food with taste has been an intriguing recent development. From Mongolian barbecues to Italian trattorias, Japanese sushi bars to Indian balti houses, the English have displayed a rare enthusiasm for the foreign experience. Yet, even though exotic food is found in every supermarket these days, and cookery programmes pollute the airwaves like a garlic burp, there are still certain dishes that remain forever England, and taste like a corner of it too. Join us for breakfast, lunch, tea, dinner and supper, as we sample the life in a day in English cuisine.

Breakfast

Good morning. Ah, no, the table is not laid for a seven course banquet - merely for the humble English breakfast: the English have traditionally liked stuffing their face of a morning. Let the French have their wee bag of air, or croissant, as they call it. A good nosh-up is unnecessary if you're going to spend all day in a café, but the English are out doing hard, manual labour in the fields. At least, they were once, and old habits die hard, especially if you're a greedy bastard.

Representatives of the muesli-loving chattering classes prefer to describe the Full English as 'a heart attack on a plate', but it retains an unmatched popularity among the nation's cholesterol addicts. Given the ease of preparation (frying pan and spatula/shovel being the only necessary cooking implements) and the unsophisticated cooking methods (fry all the items in the same pan until you can't tell them apart), it is little wonder that lazy English cooks give the Full English full rein. And little wonder that they suffer heart attacks by the million.

Any self respecting Full English includes the following: at least three rashers of bacon, two eggs, two pork sausages, mushrooms, tomatoes, fried bread and black pudding (congealed pig's blood). Offal provides an optional extra for those with a particularly strong constitution. Having forked this into his face, the traditionalist washes it down with great mugs of strong, sweet tea and mops up any walking wounded on the plate with an ambulance sized lump of bread and butter. One can begin to see why the muesli brigade feel so smug. Unsurprisingly, many Full

English breakfast devotees go on to have a series of very impressive heart by-pass operations - a shame, as some sort of stomach by-pass earlier in their careers would no doubt prevent this entirely.

Grave health warnings are ignored by the patient traditionalist, however. Given that anyone who can light a gas hob and throw lard into a pan is halfway to producing a passable Full English, it is little wonder that its popularity continues apace. It may look like a road traffic accident involving three teddy boys and a tanker of crude oil, but the Full English boasts a degree of taste that belies its appearance. The fry up may be a downright danger as a diet, but it's a good treat now and then, and very useful for absorbing hangovers, so its place (quite literally) in the traditionalist's heart looks secure.

In complete contrast are the aforementioned muesli brigade: health food fascists who grind their way through their beloved bran with barely a thought for their molars, their taste buds, or the unpleasant odours caused by fibre overload. These peculiar souls turn their nose up at the thought of fry ups, although turning your nose up becomes habitual when you visit the lavatory that regularly. What is so great about being regular anyway? The English may take pride in routine, but most of them savour a decent poo whenever they so happen to be blessed, without the need to make a timetable about it. One might claim that the muesli brigade were too anally retentive, if this didn't fly in the face of overwhelming evidence to the contrary.

Finally, toast. We are all equal under toast. Whether we are breakfasting with a hungover student, an office temp on the run or a fastidious businessman, certain time-honoured traditions are observed. The type of bread itself is irrelevant - whatever it is, it will always end up BURNT. One might assume from observation that the English like their toast black on one side and a virginal white on the other. It is not so - this is why Marmite was invented: it disguises the white side, you see, though most English attempts at toast are so inept that the Marmite ends up on the burnt parts.

Lunch

Finally, lunch rolls round. For some, this heralds round rolls, for others, several rounds of drinks and a five course meal. Sadly, the latter are a dying breed. More people are turning to the gourmet business sandwich - a generally soggy affair, packaged in plastic to stop it leaking until your trousers are in range. Meanwhile, thousands of schoolchildren are suffering the travesties that their mothers have prepared the evening before - at least, those schoolchildren who didn't fling their sandwiches all over the bus. Favourite fillings include 'some sort of paste' which tastes vaguely of sick, or 'some sort of meat' which is unnaturally round and resembles a skin graft.

In sharp contrast to these weekday snacks is the Traditional Sunday Dinner. The English meal *par excellence*, it is still consumed with enthusiasm by an impressive proportion of all classes, apart from the chattering segment of the middle class. With their progressive and ultra-modern attitudes, they snub roast lamb, beef and pork in favour of dishes containing chick peas. They don't seem to realise that chick peas are battery farmed too.

Quite why the vegetarian chattering classes should shun the Sunday Dinner is beyond comprehension, given its impressive range of vegetables. The meat, of course, provides the focal point of the dinner - its slow-roasting method suiting English patience perfectly, providing they've remembered to put it in the oven at half eleven the night before. But it is in the number of vegetables that the roast stands or falls. Carrots, cabbage, turnip or swede, peas, broad beans, broccoli, parsnips and leeks are all possibilities. Nobody likes sprouts, but they are a must in season (Christmas Day). Meanwhile, any self-respecting Sunday Dinner will boast mashed, roast and new potatoes - only the Irish can claim a greater allegiance to the spud. In addition, a chipolata or two often appears wrapped in bacon for modesty in case the vicar calls round.

This kaleidoscope of colours, smells and textures ought, in theory, to make the Sunday Dinner a delight to the taste-buds. Unfortunately, traditional cooking methods are such that the English must resort to three tried methods of resuscitating taste.

The first is to pour gravy liberally over everything, which makes for an interesting guessing game with what's on the plate. As a rule, if it's soggy, it's a vegetable; if it's hard, it's a potato; if it's leathery, that'll be the meat; and if it's brown and manages all three in one go, it's just the gravy.

The second is to dollop generous helpings of sauces onto the meat: horseradish for beef; mint for lamb; apple for pork. Finally, mustard is used everywhere, but younger brothers find it most effective hidden in their sister's dessert.

The third is stuffing, though this is really only applied to poultry, which is cooked whole, thus retaining its body cavity for the purpose. The art of good stuffing has been all but lost - but help is at hand with the pre-made variety. Mind you, it looks like a piece of mattress, and is probably best used for stuffing one.

Still, the food itself is hardly the main point to the Sunday Dinner - it's the gathering of the family on the holy day. Families across the country are united, weeping. Is this a surfeit of piety from the morning visit to church? No, someone has mixed mustard into the sherry. Dinner commences in stony silence, or with recriminations and abuse flying, along with the odd spud. Some are praying. Praying for humility? No, praying that little brother develops CJD from the beef, or salmonella from the chicken (though cancer from their burnt potatoes is far more likely). Then the men stagger away to sleep off their five lunchtime pints, the women sag in a sherry stupor and arguments over the washing-up break out to wile away the afternoon until tea time.

Tea

For the aristocracy and middle classes, tea is a mid to late afternoon affair, while the working class swill it all day long. The aristocracy eat cucumber sandwiches with theirs, but with all the filling bits, like the bread crusts and cucumber skins removed, making tea the only time of the day where the rich don't go for over-consumption. This is a sensible move, given that they will have to gnaw their way through twenty courses before bed-time.

For the middle classes, however, tea is a luxury, especially as practised by ladies of a certain ripe age, with hair of a certain ripe colour. Around three or four in the afternoon, they congregate to brew, stew and warm the pot, before daintily wolfing a plateful of cream cakes. Tea provides these women with the ideal opportunity to meet the vicar and share their concerns about the community, or meet with their cronies and backstab their neighbours. It is a ritualised affair, played out over luxury shortbreads and antique china: a show of sophistication for these bored housewives. For just these occasions, one can buy expensive sachets of herbal and flavoured teas - Willow herb and Foxglove, Lavender and Beetroot or Elderflower and Rohypnol (for the vicar). Their high colour and lack of taste are the perfect complement to this middle-class affair.

Dinner

Little has changed for the aristocracy over the centuries, dinner commencing, as ever, with the starter - a delicate slice of toast with a small pile of caviar, balanced on half a roast pig.

The same cannot be said for the rest of the country.

Gone are the days of rabbit stew, steak and kidney pudding and shepherd's pie which, for the most part, is a good riddance. Home-cooked English cuisine has gone global and any middle-class kitchen now boasts influences from countries as diverse as Italy, India, Thailand and China.

English attempts at exotic food are generally pretty poor and a distressing turn for the bland has crept into international food - especially when it comes from a supermarket freezer cabinet. For a start there seems to be an obsession with breadcrumbs - everything has to be coated in them: from pastas and curries to yoghurt sorbets.

Next, there is a strange cross-cultural interbreeding. Forget genetically modified ingredients, worry instead about paella Kiev, or chilli con Cornish pasty. If a chicken Kiev is worth eating, it should surely be on its own merits, not in some bastardised form. Luckily for the visitor, these aberrations tend to be limited to the lower middle classes, who believe them to be a cultured and cosmopolitan alternative to the usual chicken nuggets, potato waffles and microwave chips.

Let's now turn to a more traditional staple: fish. Increasing numbers of the English have become squeamish about seafood - a depressing turn for an island race. However, the great English feast of fish and chips is still holding its own against competition from burger bars and kebab shops, perhaps because the fish is disguised in a jacket of batter. The menu in a fish and chip shop usually looks like this: cod and chips; haddock and chips; mushy peas; baked beans; jumbo sausages; curry sauce; and pickled eggs, gherkins, or onions as an extra speciality. For information: mushy peas, the vegetarian option, are the surprisingly luminous result of mushing peas - the ultimate in easy eating, all you have to do is drink and digest them (more of a challenge than it sounds). Jumbo sausages only taste like elephant, and are the chippy's answer to the rotating leg in the kebab shop window. In keeping with modern trends, many chippies offer more exotic fare: kebabs, Chinese or Indian. However they're all prepared by chefs whose kitchen know-how begins and ends with the on switch of the deep fat fryer - none are recommended.

Where chippies differ from other fast food oulets, is in the eponymous chip. Visitors to England weaned on anorexic French fries are amazed to discover great slabs of greasy potato, cooked in fat to a point of saturated succulence. With these the English make chip butties - the most carbohydrate-rich delicacy in the world - by placing the chips between slices of bread and butter. For the underclass, this often provides their only form of nutrition - and explains the unique medical condition of simultaneous cellulite and scurvy. 'Scraps' - small pieces of over-fried batter - are a popular accompaniment and proof that what the English sometimes lack in heart, they make up for in heart attacks.

The English have, in their own unadventurous way, begun to embrace a variety of different foods. The catalyst for this has been the large-scale, post-colonial influx of immigrants from the Indian sub-Continent. The arrival of Indian, Pakistani and Bangladeshi chefs, waiters and restaurateurs in recent years has provided one of the most positive culinary episodes since tea was imported - showing that patience sometimes is rewarded.

Marks and Spencer, a typically English middle-class chain store, now sells 18 tonnes of chicken tikka masala a week, English football fans have an anthem called Vindaloo and curry cook-in-sauces are now as essential in the weekly shop as horseradish, mint and apple. G. K. Noon and Parveen Wassi of the Patak's curry cook-in sauces range are now on the *Sunday Times* list of England's richest people. Meanwhile, the Mumtaz brand supplies its version of Asian sauces to Harrods. In short, the curry is now part of the English establishment.

Where did curry come from? It is almost unknown in its alleged home of Asia. Historians of the curry phenomenon argue that Bangladeshi immigrants working on P&O ferries came to realise that their English passengers, unused to flavoursome food, appreciated the addition of spices to their meals. And the more spices they added, the more the English appreciated them. Sacked by their English managers for providing a modicum of customer care, they came ashore with a plan: to wake the sleepy English palate. From their first-hand experience, they understood the English tradition of covering their meals with liquid - gravy on their Sunday dinner, grease on their full English and mushy peas on their fish and chips. And so they experimented with this concept using spice - and curry was born. It was only natural that a meal with taste and swimming in sauce would succeed, and the exponential growth of curry houses is testament to the vision of the Bangladeshi pioneers.

Given the curry's history, first-time Asian visitors eating at an English 'authentic Indian' restaurant are always shocked. Their reaction is the equivalent to that of a homesick Englishman finding an 'authentic' fish and chip shop in Los Angeles, only to be served nude fish and stringy fries. The curry, then, is not authentic Indian at all - rather, a fabrication of what the English want an Indian meal to be. This is why the waiters have hours of fun disguising their Brummie, Yorkshire or Cockney accents with Peter Sellers-style impersonations of Indian English.

The first curry houses were opened in the 1970s, catering to those members of the working classes who thrived on the challenge of eating food considered by the Asians themselves to be painfully hot.

The Phal - even more excruciatingly spicy than the lethal

Vindaloo - became a staple weekend meal for young, alcoholic working-class men. Having spent an evening in the pub competing to drink the most, youths would stagger to the local curry house. There, they would subject the waiters to racist taunts, and would themselves be subjected to oral pain beyond their worst nightmares, as the amused chefs and waiters carried out their revenge. Today, curry emporia come in all shapes and sizes. Even the middle classes find the better class of curry house as convivial an environment as the garden centre or the lounge area of the pub.

Of course, while the rest of the country has picked and nibbled at these assorted dishes, the hardy aristos have ploughed through their standard 27 courses. Those still conscious are passing the port, until...

...Supper

The night is young, and there is nothing to get up for tomorrow, save a huge breakfast. Might be worth toddling along to the kitchen and seeing if we can't make a start on it now old man, get ahead of ourselves, what? Capital idea, capital. Fancy a nightcap?

Conclusion

There is only one way to round off the day's eating (urp!): pass the stomach pump, Mabel.

Nine: TRANSPORT

Trains, Buses, and Traffic Jams

In the modern world, most have the opportunity to travel privately if they want, and in a nation of excessively private people, this method is clearly preferred. Although the English invented the train, the intimacy of the car fits the national temperament like a well-crafted leather driving glove, and it has become a national obsession. Nearly every family from every class owns at least one, providing a point of focus for the competitive middle classes, alloy-wheeled boy racers, harassed commuters and chauffeured toffs alike.

Somewhere along the way the patient English have managed to transform a contraption designed to liberate and enrich into one that bankrupts and frustrates. Still, they continue to spend hours stuck in traffic jams and pounds on over-taxed petrol, because it provides them with the privacy they value so highly.

Public transport does exist in England. The poor do not own cars, and for the rest, they suffer break-downs sooner or later, or their patience snaps (incidents of 'road rage' have shown that the death of the motoring dream might finally be taking its toll on the English). Then, they travel by coach or train. The fact that the English accept a train journey from Manchester to Liverpool takes longer now than it did in 1900, is a perfect illustration of the point at which English patience crosses the line into apathy. Meanwhile, the coach and bus networks allow the English to grit their teeth publicly as they become embroiled in the traffic jam they might have sat through privately in their car.

So, how is it possible a nation can happily spend its public holidays stuck in 25-mile tailbacks? Why do English commuters jump for joy when the train is on time? How can bus drivers stay in their occupation without intensive weekly psychoanalysis?

Our answers lead us to the very heart of the English transport system, but will we be home again before bedtime?

The car

English drivers use the left hand side of the road, known to foreigners as the 'wrong' side. So visitors are often confused when they take to the English wheel. Thankfully, the snail's pace of English traffic allows the newcomer ample opportunity to acclimatise. Let us examine why English road travel is so unbearably slow, and why the visitor ought to pack Betablockers or tranquillisers before setting foot in his hire car.

The author engaged the help of a transport consultant to discuss the English roads crisis, on a footbridge over England's most famous new road, the M25, which circles London.

We arrived separately. The roar of the constant traffic was such that, when the consultant began his exposition, he was virtually inaudible and, after five frustrating minutes, we were both coughing uncontrollably from the pollution. We agreed to reconvene at a service station. Unfortunately, there are only two service stations on the M25. Luckily, we were but five miles from one of them. Unluckily, the consultant got on the wrong side of the motorway, and had to drive all the way round the other way. He still arrived half an hour before the author.

In the services' cafeteria, over muddy tea, he resumed his exposition.

"You see, the problem is that, although cars offer privacy to the traveller, they have to run on roads, which are public. No one wants more roads, but everyone wants to drive. It's a bit of a poser isn't it? The net effect, of course, is that the English spend most of their working days commuting, and their weekends and holidays crawling along motorways. And while cars become more comfortable, they don't mind doing it."

He looked around the cafeteria at the tattooed, overweight

long-distance lorry drivers, the families tending their travel sick young, and the callow sales executives comparing car stats and spilling grease over their paperwork. "You see," he observed, "they're as happy as pigs in shit."

With that, he made his excuses and left - he had another appointment three hours hence, some 15 miles away.

To put his comments in topographical context, England is just over 400 miles long and averages 200 miles in width. This is the area now used by some 20 million motorists, but it wasn't always thus. During the glorious years of the Twenties and Thirties, England had exactly the right balance of cars to roads - and a wide cross section of the public could afford to motor. The King's highways were still the stuff of rural idyll. Motoring meant freedom, and the chance to see a bit of countryside. The only previous way to experience 'the joys of the open road' was to be a tramp. It is precisely this collective golden memory that lingers in the public imagination, as evinced by increasingly ridiculous car adverts showing people driving out of traffic jams and off up mountains.

The car suits a big open country like America, where there is room to build graceful freeways, stretching for miles in straight lines. Meanwhile, most of the cramped little European countries realise the folly of trying to cram too many roads inside their borders. But not the English. Why? Can it be the old love of contradiction again?

Margaret Thatcher thought the car was a wonderful invention and felt compelled to address the problem of the congested road network with an innovative solution: laying more tarmac. She seemed to have logic on her side for once: more roads would bring more space for cars and therefore fewer traffic jams. But her judgement utterly ignored the obsessive mentality of the English driver. The more roads she had built, the more people drove on them, which wasn't really playing the game, and the new roads soon became clogged with their own congestion. Thatcher's original intent had been perverted by its own success - the policy actually increased traffic.

The present government has reached a rather different solution to the traffic problem, as the following faithful transcript of a transport policy meeting shows.

Transport Minister: I know! Let's increase the tax on petrol - that'll get them onto the buses and trains, surely.

Over-educated mandarin: An intriguing idea, minister, but we already tax petrol at a rate considerably higher than any other European nation and have done so for many years. The effect on the typical driver is to give him a cause to rally round. He feels hard done by, and continues to use his car out of sheer spite. Thus, there is a positive correlation between the rate of increase in duty and the rate of increase in numbers of cars.

Transport Minister: Well, let's build some more roads, then. More space and less jams. C'mon - the voters'll love it.

Over-educated mandarin: Another intriguing suggestion, minister, but again a bit of a no-no. Another positive correlation exists: increase road mileage and you increase traffic jam mileage too. There's more room for them, you see?

Transport Minister: Well, what do you suggest?

Over-educated mandarin: Far be it for me to initiate policy, minister, but I think we ought to let sleeping dogs lie. The motorist appears quite used to the current state of affairs. The treasury is more than happy with the 78 per cent duty on petrol and should you build more roads, the environmental lobby would be down on you like a ton of tarmacadam.

Transport Minister: Yes, I see. Well done. Business as usual, then?

Over-educated mandarin: Yes, minister. A wise and magnanimous choice, I am certain.

Allow us to escape the road for the moment and take refuge in the service station, as it features in most lengthy English car journeys. All services are equally dreadful, but there are two main brands, which, to avoid legal action we will call by their colloquial names: *The Little Shit*, and *The Crappy Eater*. Both of these roadside travesties claim to provide warm (or at least re-heated) welcomes, and a homely family atmosphere. You might find the latter to be true if you happen to live with a family of Lego people, for plasticity is king here, and that applies especially to the food. You know the cuisine is of dubious quality when even the glossy pictures on the laminated menu look awful. An unfounded rumour exists that some of these places employ a chef, though quite what he does to beguile the time is unknown. Presumably it falls to him to open the boxes and defrost the pre-packaged 'Great English Breakfasts'. 'Our chef: what that man can't do with a knife is nobody's business. Why, I saw him open a plastic carton at five paces with just a flick of his wrist the other day.'

The proprietors are clearly well-versed in the following basic economic law: 'In a monopoly market with a captive customer base, fleece 'em for all they're worth'. And so, the hungry traveller in the service 'restaurant' is faced with stark choices: £3.00 for a bowl of under-heated tomato soup and a moderately stale roll, £4.95 for the 'cheese omelette' which one suspects has been found on the road outside and tea at ten pence per tea leaf. Or starve.

Thanks to the English predilection to make do with whatever is placed before them, these shit holes will thrive until hell is defrosted. But it needn't be this way. The traditional country roadside inn is still hanging on by the skin of its beer, just behind the by-pass, and most do a reasonable imitation of pub-grub. Or else, one can (for once) benefit from the example of the English pensioner, who prepares a packed lunch before any journey of more than twenty minutes: a reminder that age can indeed bring wisdom. If only the patient English majority followed their admirable example, the services might stop ripping them off.

We have eaten, we have drunk and we have thrown up in the car park. Now let's hit the road! Who are we going to meet out there, as we struggle to move into second gear; as we marvel at the English wildlife spread out before us on the tarmac; as we laugh at the delicious irony of a 70 mile-per-hour speed limit? Well, English drivers, as we would expect in this nation of hierarchy and order, can be neatly categorised into distinct pigeon-holes.

Top of the list are those with the classiest vehicles. Rolls-Royces are really the Rolls-Royce amongst cars. Bentleys and Jaguars are also popular with the rich. To own one of these cars, all of which can run at some 15 miles to the gallon, an annual income of over a quarter of a million pounds is an absolute minimum. Drivers in this category are therefore aristocrats, high-flying members of the upper-middle class, or extremely successful criminals. They take congestion in good heart, given their vehicles' luxurious leather seats, TV sets and drinks cabinets. Drinking and driving is fine when you have your chauffeur at the wheel. Little wonder that these cars are the kings of the English road.

Tasteless new money yuppies in their sports cars provide an entirely different breed of English driver. Indeed, of the range of driving types on English roads, these are the least likely to show the patience and reserve for which the general population is rightly lauded. Constantly rushing to clinch the next deal, they are infuriated by congestion, they honk their horns (or have their secretary do it), play loud music, flash their lights and bang on their wheels in a permanent state of impatient anger. Theirs are the shortest driving careers - the Porsche exchanged at some stage for a plush helicopter, a dark prison cell or an early grave. This all depends on whether they clinch the deal, attack someone in a fit of road rage or get distracted by their mobile phone and crash into the central reservation.

The four-wheel drive has made a bizarre appearance on English roads in recent times, and is usually found among the more rurally minded sections of the middle class, though not necessarily the more rurally located. These scourges of the suburbs have become vital for traversing speed bumps and vying with other parents in the battle to have the kids at school on time. The only reason the kids don't walk to school is that the roads are too dangerously full of four-wheel drives. The bumpers on these monsters may be essential for drivers in the Australian outback, but are quite out of place in a country whose animal hazards rarely come bigger than a hedgehog. Nevertheless, their drivers are able to deal with the frustrations of congestion by looking down on virtually every other car on the road, thus giving them a much-needed sense of superiority.

'White van man' rules the city streets. Though his van is unmarked but for 'clean me' written in the dirt, the general car user recognises that he has a vastly important consignment of dodgy stereos to deliver, and lets him bend all the rules of the road, as well as lampposts, bollards and pedestrians.

The Morris Traveller is another classic addition to the English roads. This half-timbered vehicle is used by oldies, like Morris and his wife, whenever they go travelling. The GB sticker on the back is testament to their adventures in motoring as far afield as The Lake District, and the tin of congealed travel sweets explains their aging false teeth. On grassy verges, forever a part of Fifties England, quaint little couples sit with flasks in admiration of the scenery, quietly loathing each other. Old travellers never die, they just exceed their lay-by date.

Many car drivers would happily use public transport, they say, if only it were reliable. But given the state of trains and buses, they remain in their cars - after all, they're gauranteed a seat.

The bus and coach

Road-based public transport obviously suffers similar problems to the car - chronic and extreme congestion. But for its poverty-stricken users (pensioners, students and single mothers with particularly noisy babies), it enjoys two distinct advantages: someone else does the driving and it is a great deal cheaper.

Local bus travel is characterised by the set routine, set faces and the set hair of the old biddies who use it the most. As we have seen in previous chapters, the bus queue is a valuable point of contact for old women. The pavement hierarchy of the queue exists once they have struggled onto the bus, too. Each old dear has her own seat, her own acquaintance and her own script. Each takes comfort in traffic congestion, allowing her the time to discuss her nasal congestion at length with anyone who will listen.

Under the guise of respect, travellers under the age of seventy give their aged fellows plenty of room, by sitting as far away as possible, vacating the lower deck entirely on a double-decker. Young mothers are the only exception to this rule. They are expected to struggle onto the bus with their children, prams, toys and carrier bags, and then allow the biddies to coo and mollycoddle their fractious babies, all the while smiling at the barbed comments of the envious post-menopausal women, whose daughters and granddaughters are no longer speaking to them.

This gentle scene of reminiscence, baby-talk and medical complaint carried out at the top of lungs, is shattered when schoolchildren enter the picture. As we saw in chapter six, their appearance proves to be a most dreadful experience for the unsuspecting passenger. Many are prepared to go heavily into debt, spending over 90 per cent of their weekly income on a car, insurance, tax and petrol in order to avoid them. The canny pensioners, on the other hand, ensure that the children are safely in their classrooms whenever they take a trip into town. The unprepared first-timer should follow this sensible course of action.

The coach is used by pensioners, students and single mothers when they travel beyond their own localities. Given the overabundance of traffic, the coach time-tables are merely theoretical works - a point recognised by their impoverished customers, who have no choice but to accept patiently the fact that they will be late.

Despite its current prosperity, England still has a considerable number of poor people, who find themselves just above the underclass threshold and who enjoy nothing better than to visit friends and family across the country. As a result, the likelihood of enjoying two seats to oneself is small, and given the cramped conditions prevalent on the typical English coach, any traveller over 5' 6" faces an uncomfortable journey.

The physical pain, however, is nothing compared to the discomfort induced by one's travelling companion, or indeed the customer service one receives during the seemingly endless journey. The typical scene finds our traveller sitting next to an over-sized, elderly woman - verbose and obese and eager to discuss her life and times. A new-born baby is screaming on a 17 year-old mother's lap immediately behind him, and in front, two students are discussing their previous evening's fifteen pints and curry - their stories backed up by a diabolical odour. With no alternative, he must grin and bear his predicament. On a positive note, his journey will provide the necessary incentive for him to find a decent job, with enough money for him to buy a car and sit privately in a traffic jam, instead of coming face-to-face with the underprivileged English coach traveller again.

The English coach journey is interspersed - once - by the offer of refreshments. The experience of one of the author's acquaintances, Mavis, serves as a salutary example of the phenomenon of English coach refreshment.

Returning home from her great aunt's, Mavis, being financially embarrassed at the time, was forced to travel by coach. Finding a space next to a snoring, anaemic-looking young man, she opened a romantic novel and began to read.

Within an hour and three quarters of boarding, the coach departed from the sleepy country town and headed towards the motorway. Dale, a nineteen year-old trainee steward with a trainee moustache, introduced himself over the loudspeaker in a camp tone, and invited passengers to peruse the laminated menu in the net pouch on the back of the seat in front.

Mavis looked up from her romantic novel, slightly annoyed,

as the heroine, Nurse Gwendolyn, was just about to fall into the arms of the muscular and domineering Dr Gilhooey. She plucked the menu from its pouch, perused as instructed, and, like many a fly before her, settled on a bacon, lettuce and tomato sandwich, with a jam doughnut and a cup of hot chocolate to follow. Though expensive, the coach was settling into a queue, and it would be a while, she thought, before she could eat again.

Two hours and thirteen miles later, Nurse Gwendolyn and Dr Gilhooey had consummated their relationship on an operating table ('More anaesthetic, Nurse, the patient's coming to'), then Dr Gilhooey proved himself a bounder by disappearing with another nurse; Nurse Gwendolyn had attempted suicide but recovered and taken a job as a firewoman, only to fall in love fifteen years later with Dr Gilhooey after rescuing him from the car crash in which the other nurse had tragically but conveniently died. Suddenly, a red-faced and sweating Dale appeared beside her.

"Hold ups?" asked Mavis with an attempt at banter.

"No, suspenders actually. D'you want anything to eat, or can I take the weight off me feet?"

"Could I have a bacon, lettuce and tomato sandwich..." Mavis began.

"Sorry, sweetheart. No BLTs left, we've had a bit of a run on them: they're always popular, though can't think why. I always say that bacon should be left to its own devices. The same goes for a good tossed..."

"How about egg mayonnaise?"

"No, all out of them as well. Make your breath smell though, they do, and your farts."

Mavis re-examined the menu.

"The boiled ham with Dijon mustard sounds nice. I'll have one of those, please," she said, politely.

"Funnily enough, I don't know why that's on there: we've never had any ham and Dijon - funny, eh? Does sound nice, though, don't it?"

"Chicken Tikka?"

"Sold the last one yesterday to an Abba fan - you know, like their hit? 'Chicken tikka, tell me what's wrong, you're enchained by your own sorrow...' I know, silly tart. Still 'e were nice looking, like."

"What about beef and onion?"

"Did 'ave some. But a retired army chap said it reminded him of his War rations - off, in other words, so I threw 'em in the bin."

"Maybe it would be better if I asked you what you do have left."

"Doughnuts. Absolutely loads of doughnuts. Doughnuts coming out of yer ar..."

"Right," said Mavis brightly, "I'll have three jam doughnuts and a hot chocolate."

"No hot chocolate, love, supplier's gone bust. Apparently, he's run off to the Seychelles."

"Coffee?" asked Mavis, desperation creeping in.

"No."

"Coke?"

"Nope."

"!"

"I'll tell you what I 'ave got, though love. Can of diet Dr Pepper."

"Right. I'll have that, and the three doughnuts, please," said Mavis, exhausted.

Dale looked down at her with the guilty insouciance of a Doctor Gilhooey.

"When I said we had loads of doughnuts, what I meant was, one. Sorry love."

"Fine," said Mavis weakly, "whatever."

Dale turned smartly on his Cuban heels.

Mavis looked forlornly out of the window at the endless

stream of vehicles. Next to her, the snorer still snored, his hand covering what seemed to Mavis a rather large erection. "No wonder he's anaemic" Mavis idly pondered, and cheered herself with the thought of the doughnut. Dale reappeared, handing Mavis the can of diet Dr Pepper.

"Some bastard's stolen the doughnut, like," he said, "but that'll be a pound for the diet Dr Pepper, please sweetie."

The train

Until recent times, the government owned the English train system. Years of union trouble in the Seventies and Conservative neglect in the Eighties caused a decline in the railways from which they are unlikely ever to recover fully. The Tories decided to get rid of them - they'd privatise your privates given half a chance ('We feel that Britprick can run a leaner, more efficient penis for you. I'm afraid there will be cutbacks'). But when an enterprise is losing money and appears unsuited to the profit principle, finding a buyer is usually difficult. So the government was forced to bribe private investors with tax payers' money, so they could sell off what wasn't theirs to sell.

There were teething troubles with the privatised companies: small things like Connex firing half of its drivers, then wondering why it couldn't run all its services. Amazingly, however, demand for rail has gone up. This wholly unforeseen circumstance has put increasing pressure on the creaking rail system, which is 50 per cent over-capacity, and likely to stay that way, as billions of pounds worth of real estate lies between the network and expansion. Only a radical solution can save the rails, like the French method of having their entire system bombed during the War, then starting from scratch.

It is not just the commuter who is worried about the train's insecure future - perhaps more anxious is the celebrated English 'trainspotter'. Trainspotters spot trains. Easy - you may think, they're big enough to see after all. However, it's details such as the name of the train, its number, its colour, the time it was spotted and the station in which it was spotted, that they're after.

"To say that trains are our life would not be overstating the case," one young trainspotter confided to the author on a windy platform at Doncaster station in south Yorkshire. "If it was possible to consummate my relationship with a diesel loco, I'd jump at the chance," he added wistfully, as he cross-referenced some numbers.

The lack of investment in the train system shames the nation. When running on time, on glistening tracks, with space to sit down, the train is the most civilised form of transport known to man. It is certainly faster and more comfortable than travel by road. Inter-city trains can reach a maximum speed of 125 miles per hour, which even the most impatient of yuppie drivers can rarely hope to match. Yet, they do not work like this - rather they provide yet another example of how the English can view incompetence, farce and disaster as part of an ordered social system. During a recent strike by those Connex staff who hadn't been sacked, passengers didn't even notice that industrial action was being taken at all.

Part of the problem, like the roads, is age. The railways were built during the nineteenth century and have not really been modernised since. During that century - a period of English industrial might - the entire country felt that man was at last conquering his natural habitat. Steam trains raced through the open countryside as peasants, ploughing the fields, fell over into their furrows in amazement, to exclaim, "At last, man is conquering his natural habitat". The great civil engineer Isambard Kingdom Brunel was laying rails of his own width, which enabled trains to corner fast. His railway architecture was graceful and glorious, and the English establishment said, "We can't have this. Make the rails thinner for God's sake." So the entire country now runs on stingy gauge.

The train is often seen as the most romantic form of travel. James Bond frequently used the train in his movies, and between bouts of athletic love-making to his gourgeous, nymphomaniac woman, he would defeat the powers of evil. But James only used trains travelling through continental Europe, where they are stylish, reliable and supported by huge government subsidies. Moreover, 007 was involved in counter-espionage and passionate love-making to beautiful women - activities which tend to break the tedium of a long journey. He was not, for instance, aboard the 17.42 commuter train from London King's Cross to Croydon, packed with bored and sweaty office clerks. For English trains to approach a level of comfort and reliability demanded by Bond, the government would need to invest heavily in infrastructure and rolling stock. But, as we have mentioned, the government has given the trains away.

Conclusion

Every mode of transport is overcrowded, out of date and overpriced. But what of the future? Is there any chance of change? Well, when the deputy prime-minister who bangs on about rail use has been nicknamed 'Two Jags', not a chance in a service station.

Ten: SPORT

Win or lose? No. Let's go for the draw

The English have been responsible for many useful inventions that are taken for granted by the modern world: Sir Isaac Newton famously invented gravity after an apple landed on his head one summer afternoon in the seventeenth century, and a very useful tool it has proved to be. It is generally agreed that, without it, the world would be a much less comfortable and ordered place than it is today. Representative democracy first flourished in the fertile political soil of England. This idea has proved an extremely popular export, except in those states that know English politics best - her former colonies - where one-party dictatorships and military oppression are felt to be a more natural progression from imperial rule.

England, historically a nation of exporters, has always been happy to share its inventions - but too often its tragedy is that *other* nations have made them work properly. The English are therefore left watching from the wings, considering what went wrong as others steal the show.

Among these manifold exports are various sports, which arguably offer the best example of how foreigners have improved upon English ideas. England is obsessed with sport: the newspapers devote more space to it than any other subject and yet its national teams never win anything of note. The population at large is constantly hopeful of success, and their teams fail in the three sports that the English consider to be theirs: football, cricket, and, to a lesser extent, rugby. It seems that, when it comes to invention, the English are only really good at creating their own humiliation. Why are things so bad?

Soccer

The game of soccer must rank as *the* truly international sport: played on all six continents by men and women alike. And, if we really are being monitored by intelligent life from space, it is probably arguing about the offside rule, too. The author met Jurgen, a German football commentator, to garner foreign opinion on the English game. These were his comments.

"England's national game is soccer. You're obsessed with it - almost as much as with your victory over Germany in 1966. How right your sporting mantra proved to be: 'They think it's all over'. Indeed it was, you've never been the best since.

"The way you play the game is hard for a German to comprehend, because we have no sense of humour, you know? It seems to be a compromise between German efficiency and Brazilian flair. But you don't know which way to turn. Your players are not skilful enough to perform as the Brazilians, and not adequately disciplined to play as we do. As a result, you rarely score, and you give away ridiculous goals. You either need to give free rein to your attackers, or tell your defenders to tighten up at the back. Until you do, the English national soccer team will be derided by the top ten international soccer-playing nations.

"And you certainly need to learn to take penalties. Ha! Ha! Ha!"

His final comment is a reference to England's record in penalty shoot-outs. During three of their last four major championships - the World Cup of 1990, the European Championships of 1996 and the World Cup of 1998 - English players just managed to secure honourable draws against clearly superior opponents. They then lost by failing the apparently simple task of scoring from 12 yards with only the goalkeeper to beat.

Hmm, so much for Jurgen. Is he right? We'll trace our way up to the present day.

Originally the game was called football - thanks to the linguistic invention of England's peasants, who liked to kick the ball with their feet. A standard version of the game probably developed from the strange inter-village chasing games, usually involving a cheese, that were popular all over the country in the Dark Ages. The English peasantry enjoyed chasing cheese all over the dung-covered fields where they had toiled for fifteen hours during the day. Village faced village across a field of corn, then promptly destroyed it with their daft shenanigans - the losing side having to eat the cheese afterwards. Eventually, facing a huge famine, the aristocracy banned them from using their fields, and the peasants were forced to play on village greens. Rules quickly followed, and an inflated bladder was introduced as a ball, saving the world from the game of footcheese, and the 200-a-side team was whittled down to eleven.

By the mid-nineteenth century, football had developed into the game that soccer is today. The game was given the name 'soccer', not when the players started wearing socks, but when the governing body of the English game was formed. The Football Association was abbreviated to the Football Assoc., and Assoc. was then colloquiallised into soccer. Its historical roots ensure soccer a place in the nation's culture and inspire the modern game with plenty of absurd behaviour.

Here we examine three areas of the contemporary game: the playing style of the English national team, the unnatural obsession of the average supporter and the cosmopolitanism of the English Premier League.

As we have argued, the generous English have exported soccer near and far. The upshot of this altruism has been that countries both near (France), and far (Brazil), play the game with greater sophistication, skill and style than the English. Their particular national characteristics - French flamboyance and the

Brazilian sense of rhythm - are given full rein on the field. By contrast, the English side plays the game according to its own national character trait - patience. Here is the generic pre-match team-talk from the English manager:

"Now then, lads. This is how we play the game. If they don't score, they can't beat us, now can they? It's bloody easy this game! If they don't score, we get at least a bloody draw out of 'em. Think about it. So, what do we do? We don't let 'em score!"

The players sit in silence, thinking: "We won't let 'em score, boss. If we can keep 'em to nil-nil, it'll be a right result. Sod the fancy stuff. Let's keep it nice and simple. And if we squeeze a late winner, all the better."

Other national teams as geographically distinct as Argentina, Cameroon and South Korea have consistently delighted neutral audiences with their rather different attitude to the game. Their managers, wildly shouting and screaming at their prima donna players, give the following instructions before their own international games:

"We score more goals than them, we win. Goals, goals, goals. Attack them. Pass the ball, show off your skills. We don't give a screw if they get some lucky goals. Let's just score more than them and we win. This game is easy - simple. Go out and score, boys."

The players dance around the dressing room, strumming their guitars, playing their castanets, and singing: "We love this game. It's a beautiful game. We can win this game if we score many goals."

Unfortunately for neutral spectators, the English approach to the game - that combination of apprehension, common sense and lack of imagination - often succeeds: England rarely score more than one goal. But neither do they let many in, contrary to Jurgen's view. Dedicated English soccer fans deal with this by calling on their infinite levels of patience. For those hoping to be entertained, however, the experience of watching England is duller than staring at a recently emulsioned wall.

This negative approach has, of course, undermined true success, as Jurgen rightly pointed out. England can confidently play any team in the world, it's true. They can reasonably expect to pull off a 'moral victory' by not allowing the Brazilians to score. But in important games, their inability to score themselves leads to the penalty shoot-out - and here the lack of confidence in their abilities, their defensive mindset and their sheer terror in front of the goal are shown up for all the world to judge. With a win or lose chance, they fail, leaving the fans the bitter disappointment of 'so near and yet so far'. No wonder Jurgen's observations nearly reduced the author to tears.

The typical English soccer fan is not the stereotype of the

hooligan, whose only form of self-expression is carnage and violence. This specimen is a tiny-brained, tiny minority whom most sensible, law-abiding fans would like to see locked up and tortured in foreign jails. But the typical English fan does demonstrate his own particular brand of irrationality. We would not expect any repressed Englishman to wear his heart on his sleeve, and share overwhelming passions with his mates in public, but this is precisely how the English soccer fan behaves. At matches, the English fan gives full vent to his frustrated love, and hitherto mild-mannered men will scream, sing, holler and weep as if insane.

The English fan's relationship with his soccer team is similar to the average Englishman's relationship with his wife. He fell in love when he was young and didn't know any better, he is stuck with her for life, even though he doesn't like her very much, but at weekends she can still make him feel like the most special man in the world.

However, unlike his wife, the soccer fan talks about his team all the time. Key topics of conversation range from analysis of his team's recent performances, to mindless statistics of his favourite players. Conversations usually last upwards of three hours and, as the lager intake rises, they descend into the slow and laboured slurring of favourite football chants.

Given his total obsession, it is impossible for the English soccer fan to see the problems faced by the national team in a cool, detached and rational manner. He takes each game in isolation, truly believing that the nation's representatives will win something. Unfortunately, 1966 appears to have been a statistical aberration, and it seems abundantly clear that England needs something more than luck before it claims top spot again. The English will, however, patiently wait - and their team will continue to disappoint.

The English Premier League has begun to tackle the

entertainment problems posed by the defensive, dour and tedious methods of the native players. Having exported the game over a century ago, the English are now using the free trade in players to import professionals who can actually play soccer properly. London-based Chelsea, for instance, regularly fields ten foreign players in its starting line-up. Few of the team's supporters can actually pronounce their player's names, but they delight in the imports' ambitious back-heels, outrageous bicycle kicks and daring flick-ups in their own penalty area. The English Premier League is therefore not really an English institution at all, and those fans who have patiently waited for flair and unremitting entertainment have indeed been handsomely rewarded.

The English Premier League is considered to be the best in the world, with an ideal mix of obsessed supporters, historical traditions and - at last - skilful players. For a country opposed both to foreigners and change, this is indeed revolutionary. As we might expect, however, the improvements in the domestic league are unlikely to affect the relative success of the national team - as so very few of the home-grown players are now good enough to get into their own English sides.

Cricket

For some, the word 'cricket' makes no sense unless preceded by the word 'Jiminy'. But for many around the globe - especially the ex-British colonies - it is a thriving and exiting game. To appreciate the foreign viewpoint of those who invented it, the author spoke to Courtney, from Antigua in the West Indies. He smiled with a knowing superiority and launched into an assault on the woes of English cricket.

"You English, you think you is the best players, because you has the best grounds and because you has been playing for many, many years, right? Well, you no got the skill now. You can't face the fast bowling, right? My friend, your batsmen is too scared to face the real ting. The West Indies, Australia, South Africa. You no can take it when we bowl fast. There's no easy wicket, soft grass or medium-pace when you come to the Windies. It's a man's game back home and we got you white boys beat..."

Courtney reclined in his seat to bask in the glow of his well-reasoned argument. The English cricket team does indeed struggle against all international opposition - and particularly against fast bowling. The author, stifling another sob, quietly thanked Courtney for his input.

In the West Indies, cricket may be a fast-paced beach game, but for the patient English, it means standing around for hours dressed in a silly white costume doing almost nothing... or sitting around for hours watching men dressed in silly white costumes doing almost nothing.

For all its eccentricities, the English version of soccer is sane in comparison to cricket. All twenty-two players are involved in soccer at all times, the match is over within an hour and a half, and the fans - though unhealthily obsessed with their teams - do not spend an entire week watching one game, only for it to be declared a draw.

The essence of cricket is to score runs (if you are a batsman) and to get wickets (if you are a bowler). If you are a fielder, the essence is to stay awake. If you are one of the nine batsmen on the batting team whose services are not currently required, the essence is to fall asleep in the changing room. Of the twenty-two players theoretically involved in the game, only three are ever directly involved - two batsmen and the bowler. The wicket-keeper keeps one eye on the game, while the non-striking batsman keeps one hand on his box. For the rest, there is literally nothing to do.

To add a touch of comedy to the proceedings, some of the fielders are given strange names, which, contrary to first impressions, do not refer to their state of physical or mental health. 'Short leg', 'long leg' and 'silly mid-on' are examples of these extraordinary titles. In addition, batsmen are expected to constantly adjust their 'box' which protects their genitals, while convention dictates that the bowler 'shines' the red ball on his trousers next to his groin. The impression that cricketers just can't stop playing with themselves is therefore entirely justified.

Surrounding the field, a number of spectators lie prostrate on itchy, woollen blankets, slowly gorging themselves on their picnics. They occasionally turn to watch the batsmen and bowlers playing with themselves. Even less frequently, a mellow ripple of applause accompanies something interesting - like a really good bit of pork pie. Some members of the audience take along a scorebook, and are engrossed all day, marking down every single event of the day's play, often using different coloured pens for individual players - then collapsing from sunstroke.

Up in the commentary box, the commentators amuse themselves by eating cake, swapping anecdotes about cake and thanking female listeners for sending in their cakes.

Cricket games take an absolute minimum of one day to complete, while international test matches take five days. After this sporting marathon, or holiday, the usual result is - yes, only the English could have devised this conclusion - a draw. Honourable, safe, but ultimately unsatisfying.

In order to garner a realistic picture of the life of a cricketer, the author sent a questionnaire to a number of professionals, asking them to describe the essence of the game. Here are the two responses:

1. 'Writing this on Saturday afternoon during the middle of another prolonged shower. The game started on Thursday morning and so far we've played for half an hour. Patience, my friend, patience is the essence of our national game.'

In this instance, the correspondent mentions the

comparatively small amount of play, given the length of the game. This is explained by the fact that rain, or even 'bad light', is reason enough for the umpires to dictate that play must stop. Given that rain and cloud are recurrent features of the English climate, the choice of cricket as a national game appears hugely optimistic and, some might say, inappropriate.

2. 'If I can just get my average up to around 39.5, I think I might have a chance of making the England 'B' touring side to Sri Lanka this winter. I know last year I managed 45.23, but this time my bowling figures - with an average of 27.83 and a strike rate of a wicket every 9.3 overs - may just carry me through.'

Given that cricketers spend the majority of their lives sitting in the dressing room, waiting for the rain to stop or nervously adjusting their boxes before they go out to bat, they become immersed in the statistics of the game. Their batting and bowling averages become the most important figures in their lives - even more important than those of their long-suffering wives and girlfriends. They compare their averages to those of their fellow players, to players from history, to their averages as schoolboys and to the fictional characters in their pepperpot cricket games which they play with spoon and cruet set on the floor of the dressing room.

So English cricket is a game dominated by statistics and delays. Does this have any effect on the way the English national team performs? And is it really as bad as Courtney described?

As we saw from the two responses to the questionnaire, English cricketers are patient, and obsessed with the minutiae of the game. This translates on the pitch into an over-cautious pedantry eschewed by other nations. The contrast could not be clearer from a comparison between Australian and English coaching methods. Australian batsmen are told that the forward defensive (a negative stroke designed to gain no runs) is 'the shot of a desperate drongo, a last resort'. English batsmen, by contrast, are ordered to rely on it. As a result, the characteristic English batsman simply 'puts his head down' and tries to 'play himself in' for hours and hours, while his opponents reach the crease with one thing on their minds - scoring runs.

All this means, of course, that the English spectator relishes the appearance of the West Indies, Australia, India, Pakistan and Sri Lanka on their native soil. Watching players who are prepared to take risks, who take pride in hitting the ball out of the ground and who believe cricket is a game of attack rather than defence comes as a welcome relief. Little wonder, then, that the internal county championship games rarely boast audiences of more than a few bored pensioners. The test matches, by contrast, attract sell-out crowds of many thousands, who throng to Lords, Trent Bridge and The Oval to see how the game should be played by the foreign experts.

As inventors of the game, for a short spell the English were the best in the world. Then the former colonies learned how to play, and England was quickly relegated to a position near the bottom of the international league. From time to time, the English do win matches. For example, in the summer of 2000, they conquered Zimbabwe and the West Indies. However, this is hardly usual (the latter victory was their first over the Windies in over 30 years) and the most the England team can usually expect is to draw a series of test matches. (Here we see the concept of the draw taken to even more absurd lengths: after six matches of five days each, it is still possible for neither side to win.)

Despite consistent failure, the doughty English cricket-loving public continues to argue that it is only a matter of time before their representatives on the field strike fear once again into the hearts and minds of their Australian, Caribbean and South African opponents. Indeed, this attitude is a pervasive feature of English national life: the optimistic assumption that England will one day regain its ascendancy in those pursuits which are now more successfully practised elsewhere. This feeling must be treated with sensitivity by visitors, especially those from richer and more successful countries. Offence might be taken at a comment like:

"I see the cricket team lost again this week. After losing your military and industrial supremacy, I suppose it must be really difficult to accept that you can't even win a cricket game."

The inaccurate belief that England remains a superior cricket nation is still prevalent at the Marylebone Cricket Club (MCC), based at the Lords ground in London. Known as 'the home of cricket', it is populated by whiskered ex-public schoolboys, who proudly wear the club's distinctive tie (a garish yellow and red diagonal stripe known as 'the eggs and bacon') along with their uniform of Panama hats and blazers. On warm summer afternoons, these representatives of the cricket establishment generally sleep on the wooden benches in front of the pavilion, waking only to shuffle slowly towards the Members' Bar to order a large, restorative G&T. The MCC is representative of the cricket tradition in England: conservative, lazy and out-of-touch. If the patient English supporter is ever to be rewarded with long-term success in the international arena, his cricketers will have to wake up and move onto the front foot.

Rugby

The game of rugby is one of the few sports in which England has enjoyed international success during recent times. The author spoke to Barry, a former Australian diplomat spending his retirement visiting places he had already visited during his diplomatic career. Barry had other ideas.

"Rugby is the national sport here, sport. The home of the game's at Twickenham, right? Well, mate, I'll tell you something for free: you English boys just can't cut it with the southern hemisphere sides any more. Fair dinkum, you always give it your best shot, but you can't play the running game like we can down south. You may have invented it, but we perfected the bugger for you…" - by which he meant the game, not what happens in the scrum. The author thanked him cordially, then tried to convince himself that, like the other foreigners he'd spoken to, he was talking out of his arse.

For once, England's international success in this arena is indisputable, but it has been achieved by restricting the annual international championship to a select few nations, which exclude the world's best teams, Australia, New Zealand and South Africa. The traditional English attribute of not taking chances - kicking the ball whenever possible, rather than passing it - gives them a fighting chance against less heavyweight rugby nations such as Ireland and Italy. And even the French often fail to deal with the dull proficiency of their English opponents.

The English rugby team is spurred on by a largely middle class crowd who provide one of the most bizarre features of international sport: repressed, Barbour-clad middle Englanders singing the black slave anthem, *Swing Low, Sweet Chariot*, at Twickenham. The tendency for rugby players to hail from the middle and upper classes is an enormous help to post-match interviewers. Whereas working-class English soccer players are about as able to string two words together as they are two passes, the representatives of the rugby side are eloquent and interesting interviewees. They often use words of four or five syllables - barely minutes after they have bitten off an opponent's ear, or stamped on the side of his head. The national rugby team is a source of inspiration and pride, and rightly so. At least until they're roundly slaughtered by teams from the southern hemisphere.

Other sports

The English do play a number of other sports. They are

knocked out in the early rounds at Wimbledon, they miss out on the major golfing titles and they sometimes manage a bronze in the Commonwealth Games. From time to time a sporting hero emerges. Linford Christie became the fastest man in the world, working against the huge handicap to aerodynamics which he kept in his shorts. Tim Henman looked like he might become one of the world's top tennis players, and then he lost to a host of players outside the top 50. Frank Bruno challenged to become the heavyweight boxing champion of the world, and then met Mike Tyson.

When the English do win at sport, the nation finds itself in a state of collective euphoria, and the newspapers report that the long-awaited Renaissance of England's international sporting prowess has arrived. This unusual state of national pride quickly fades when the English return to the more common state of losing, or eking out a draw, and the Renaissance is quietly forgotten . . . until the next time.

Given England's long and distinguished tradition of inventing sports, its recent international performances are indeed a disappointment to a patient nation. However, two sports offer solace to a people searching desperately for victory. These are darts and snooker. Unfortunately, many commentators argue in persuasive terms that these activities are games rather than sports. One of their number, who wished to remain anonymous on the reasonable grounds that he is a sports commentator specialising in darts and snooker, offered the following rationale:

"Let's face it, we'd be better off describing darts and snooker as 'unhealthy pastimes' rather than 'sports'. Neither of them requires an iota of physical fitness. In fact, they're played almost exclusively in pubs and working men's clubs and the competitors all drink and smoke while they play. A walk to the bar has them gasping for breath. If they're sportsmen, I'm a gorilla."

Although this line of argument holds a certain attraction with the author, it must be discounted. England has enjoyed so little success in recent years that the nation's self-esteem absolutely requires darts and snooker to be classified as sports. Without their contribution, the national sporting trophy cabinet would be almost bare.

Although most contestants in these two sports are English, stacking the odds does not always achieve the desired result. In the 2000 Embassy world snooker championships, for instance, the final was fought out by two Welshmen. But, on the whole, both darts and snooker give the English a fighting chance which, as the preceding argument has demonstrated, is more than can be said for other more athletic spheres.

Conclusion

English sport reveals the nation's ability to accept inevitable defeat and disappointment as but a temporary blip which will soon end in triumph and glory. Sport is both a symptom and a cause of obsessive pedantry, trundling mediocrity and, in the case of soccer hooligans and rugby players, violent thuggery. Despite the English invention of the world's most popular sports, its contemporary players and supporters find victory elusive and defeat a regular fact of life. But here, as elsewhere, the English prove they are champions of the world in one vital sphere: patience.

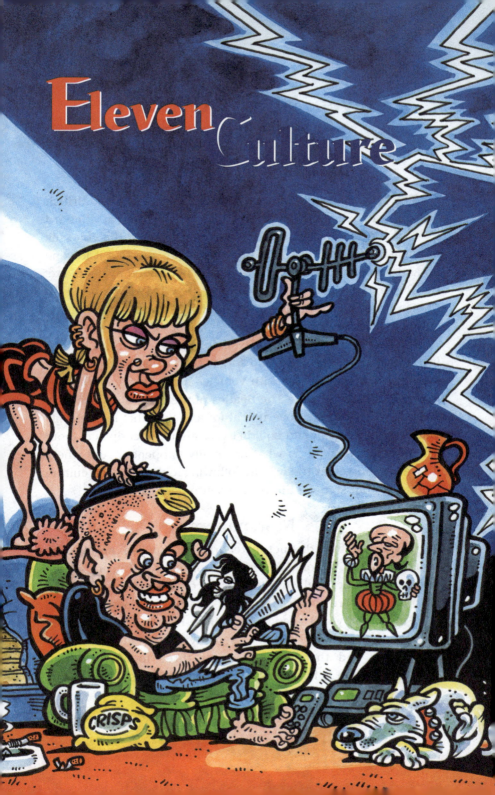

Eleven: NEWSPAPERS, TV AND THE ARTS

The cultural health of the English patient

The Times of London, William Shakespeare, the British Broadcasting Corporation, Noël Coward, Richard Attenborough. Such names once formed the colossus of English culture which bestrode the world, and had it looking up and thinking, 'My! What balls!' Their modern equivalents are: the Rupert Murdoch press empire, Andrew Lloyd Webber, BBC Choice, Noel Edmonds, Richard and Judy. These have England sitting in a stupor thinking, 'My! What bollocks!'

Where did it all go wrong? Well, it is easy, of course, to look favourably upon the past, and forget that William Shakespeare started his writing career with vehicles for *Johnny and The Hey Nonny Players*, who were The Beatles of their day. It is also easy to blame the Thatcher government for a society that increasingly values material gain, and couldn't give a stuffed codpiece about artistic improvement. So what has really happened? And where do we find ourselves today? The following look at English culture might help put some of these trends into perspective.

Newspapers

There are two distinct categories of English newspaper: broadsheet and tabloid. To read the former you'll need: a keen interest in politics and world events, an obtuse mind to solve the cryptic crossword and five foot arms - to fold the bloody thing. To read the latter you'll need; to find bare breasted women more interesting than news, a lack of sensitivity to being patronised mercilessly and the slightly smaller three foot arms more commonly found in humans. Our analysis provides further proof of the class-consciousness of English society, and shows exactly why the second category of newspaper sells so many more copies than the first.

Despite their inconvenient size and content, broadsheets can claim a loyal and large readership. Among the upper ranks of society, this can be attributed to its daily cryptic crossword. The aristocracy love to wile away the hours with the day's mind-bender, flattering themselves with the knowledge they share a mind-set with the obtuse university don who created it. There are those in the lower classes who enjoy the crossword too, but they are just clever, completing it as an afterthought, having already gone from cover to cover and penned several letters to the editor. Nevertheless enormous social cachet is attached to the ability to complete these puzzles, such is the English love of perversity and secret rules.

As we have already suggested, the broadsheets tend to concentrate their energies on that dullest of subjects: politics. This provides them with another wellspring of readers - the chattering classes. Generally speaking, the only people interested in politics are politicians, and even that's no given. But there is also that dwindling number of people with a social conscience, who ease it by reeling off statistics and one-sided arguments about world debt, unemployment, inflation and the size of the underclass.

Politicians the world over appear in their country's newspapers by dint of the fact that they wield power. For instance, General Tutone-Cupé of Guacamala regularly appears on the front page of the *Tutone-Cupé Bugle*, or else thumbs are broken.

In England politicians have absolutely no power at all, thank goodness. As a result, they can only gain the illusion of power when their members' bills are reported at length in the broadsheets, or when their sexual peccadilloes make the front page of a tabloid. The latter method is more fun, especially for those junior ministers who mistake a peccadillo for an armadillo, and achieve notoriety beyond their wildest dreams. We shall return to the subject of politics in a later chapter. Suffice it to say that broadsheets have boosted English politicians' egos for centuries, while tabloids have boosted English politicians' sex lives for decades.

The broadsheet is so called not just for its breadth of size, but for its scope and depth of subject. Its several acres of newsprint mean that it can simultaneously provide in-depth political analysis, coverage of world events, home news, culture, finance, lifestyle, travel and sport. It is also useful for covering a tabloid or naughty magazine.

The well-dressed, prosperous-looking gent on the train home can sit looking smug as he wields his broadsheet to the detriment of those either side of him. Wriggling in his seat with a repressed smile on his lips, he certainly seems to be enjoying his parliamentary report rather too much. Is something up? Something certainly is: hidden from the prying eyes of fellow passengers behind the staid broadsheet is a copy of *Aspects of Aspic*, the jelly fetishist's favourite.

As long as commuter camouflage is needed, the broadsheet should enjoy a safe future, regardless of its editorial matter.

We now examine the tabloid, the medium which truly puts the tit in titillation and the naked nipple on every news counter in the country. Broadsheets may account for the bulk of newsprint used in England, but the tabloid accounts for the bulk of the reading population. We say 'reading population', but basic literacy is superfluous to the enjoyment of a tabloid - banner headlines and half-naked women are the key ingredients here. Below we offer a summary of the tabloid's contents.

1. A page of gratuitous opinion on one main item of 'news' (often Royalty related).

2. Several pictures of women in a variety of G-strings and thongs.

3. A column devoted to sexual problems such as transvestism, trans-sexualism, impotence, adultery, venereal disease, unplanned pregnancies, sado-masochism and nymphomania.

4. The stars - or horoscopes - which offer the various Geminis, Librans, and Sagittarians false hope of alleviating the seemingly intractable problems addressed in the sexual problem column.

5. Fabricated stories about celebrities fighting, being arrested, having sex, being drunk and disorderly, coming out of the closet and being broke, usually all in one evening.

6. Amazing revelations of ordinary people doing extraordinary things.

A random sample of *The Sun*, analysed under strictly scientific conditions, featured photographs of five pairs of naked breasts (along with their owners), and another two nubile girls lying provocatively on a beach - all between pages one and three. Also between these pages was half a column inch of detailed discussion on the Queen's latest frock, and its implications for the future of the monarchy. Meanwhile, a two-page spread discussed a soccer star's alleged alcoholism. The 'Women's Section' included a guide on how to tell if you have breast cancer (featuring a naked woman feeling her own breasts). An 'EXCLUSIVE', so called because no-one else would touch it, detailed the 'SEXPLOITS' of a holiday rep. who'd 'bedded' at least 1,200 women during his four years on Tenerife. In the stars, the problem of the day chronicled the sad story of a Virgo whose girlfriend was being unfaithful to him at the stables where she worked. The tactful and sensitive advice from the astrologer-cum-psycho-sexual counsellor was: 'Use your Virgoan strength to get rid of this stable girl as she obviously needs a stallion to satisfy her.'

Indeed all 6 characteristics listed above were present in this randomly selected example. Whether this should be a cause for national concern is an issue for some debate. Some claim that the topless girl on page three is a national institution. Others argue that a set of boobs doth not a national institution make, but this overlooks the Royal Family somewhat.

There is just one tabloid which doesn't follow the puerile, exploitative model outlined above, one that stands out as a shining beacon of common sense and family morality, one intelligent enough for readers who have put down the deposit for a mind of their own, and genuinely believe they might one day own it. This bastion of the middle-middle classes is *The Daily Mail*. *The Mail* is an important organ of the press: we know this because it tells us so itself. And it is right: no-one else does more to keep the middle-middles cowering in their homes, too scared to venture outside in case they encounter a teenage single mother prostitute with AIDS cracked out of her head on jizz sugar. *The Mail*, with its rampant, paranoid fear of crime, sex, sexuality, culture, change and difference has caught the mood of Middle England perfectly. Little wonder its readers are so miserable.

Television

The focus of our discussion now turns to the popular medium of television. Until recently, like Iraq, China and Saudi Arabia, English screens were dominated by state television (the BBC). The English patiently listened to the news presenters' cut glass Queen's English and watched class-based drama serials like *Upstairs, Downstairs* and adaptations of nineteenth century novels by Charles Dickens and Jane Austen.

The traditional English antipathy towards choice and their love of bureaucracy ensured that they were more than happy to buy their TV licences, which paid for the salaries of well-spoken presenters and the lavish sets for the period dramas. Today, the picture is a little fuzzier. We find the BBC desperately trying to justify the licence fee in the face of intense competition from both domestic commercial stations and satellite channels. Let us therefore examine the contemporary scene.

One of the BBC's chief strengths is its lack of advert interruptions during programmes. The one serious drawback to this popular policy is the lack of opportunity to make a cup of tea or relieve oneself during the transmission. However, specifically for this purpose the ever considerate BBC provides programmes featuring right-wing comic has-been, Jim Davidson.

Your licence fee buys you two terrestrial BBC channels: BBCs 1 and 2. BBC2 is noted for its sensitive and interesting transmissions on subjects as diverse as opera, the world population crisis and alternative comedy. BBC1 is noted for animal programmes, awful game shows and soap operas. The animal programmes are particularly popular with the English audiences, who take curious pleasure in watching wildebeest being devoured by hungry lions as they themselves tuck into their dinner. Being a nation of animal lovers, the English are also fond of watching animals in pain on the increasingly numerous vet programmes which infest TV schedules these days. Time was when the innocent pleasure of a man with his hand up a puppet would suffice. Now, if its not a Labrador with a rectal carcinoma, no-one wants to know.

The BBC rightly has a reputation for fair and comprehensive news coverage, though the majority of English viewers do not tune in until the weather forecast at the end. However, when a national disaster such as the death of Princess Diana strikes, the nation sits agog before the hourly bulletins. During such times of crisis, the BBC has proved its expertise in reflecting the national mood - a sensitivity which went out of the window, thank God, during Di Fortnight. While the hysterical hordes outside wept and tore out their hair, the newsreaders simply donned professionally impartial faces and sombre black clothing (though one weather forecaster was clearly unprepared for national mourning, and had to resort to a velvet smoking jacket several sizes too small).

One of the BBC's most serious problems of late has been the loss of its renowned sporting coverage to less proficient and often downright incompetent rivals. This is most painfully illustrated by the defection of England's best sporting presenter, the smooth and sophisticated Desmond Lynam, to ITV. And from the FA Cup Final to six nations rugby, from cricket test matches to the Grand Prix, the BBC has meekly rolled over and allowed commercial television to steal its thunder. Yet, amazingly, it still manages to trample all over its summer schedules with extended sports coverage. Now that's professionalism for you.

The BBC is still a quintessentially English institution, retaining its stiff upper lip in the face of enormous corporate competition and allowing its rivals to take its customers. The

BBC is hardly likely to go out of business. After all if you own a TV set, you must, by law, buy a licence. So, in true paternalistic form, it produces programmes it believes the nation *should* watch instead of those it wants to watch. And, like most fathers, it underestimates the age of its charges, and serves up bland pap when many would prefer something to get their teeth into.

The main terrestrial commercial channel is ITV, which has been on the English airwaves since before BBC2. Where once ITV tried to ape the quality of BBC, and occasionally succeeded, the roles have been reversed and perverted. Now the BBC apes the low quality of ITV. Unfortunately, they're now both as bad as each other with their tacky game shows, soap operas, fly-on-the-wall documentaries and DIY programmes.

A well-known game show formula is unashamed exuberance and emotional openness from the contestants. To provide riveting entertainment, they are expected to applaud themselves, cry, scream, jump up and down, faint and act in a most uncouth manner. To this end, small electrodes are placed on their chairs. Now, if only someone could do the same to the cretinous hosts, game shows might be worth watching.

The fly-on-the-wall documentary provides a 'private' glimpse into the world of the English home. The programme-makers clearly aim for a middle-class audience, so they film the working class and underclass, and, from fifty hours of footage, half an hour of the worst bits are edited together and served up to a credulous TV audience as reality. This gives viewers the opportunity to feel even more smug and superior about their tidy homes and tidy lives. Unfortunately, like a real fly on the wall, after ten minutes trapped in a room with it, you have an uncontrollable urge to smash your head repeatedly against the window.

DIY and gardening makeover programmes naturally find a huge and dedicated following of devotees among a similar audience. Except this time, it is the middle class who star. This is why you never see Carol Vorderman (professional TV presenter at large) making a water feature out of a rusting Ford Capri. Instead, simpering couples struggle to hold back tears as their dream of a tasteful new sitting room is realised. Their life's ambition fulfilled, these soulless morons should, by rights, take themselves out into the garden and drown themselves in the ornamental pond.

Channel Four is a bastion of the avant-garde and intellectual. Indeed, its reputation for producing thought-provoking material for the chattering classes to discuss during their dinner parties challenges that of BBC2. When Channel Four was launched, it showed a number of erotic foreign films that attracted a wide audience of breast-obsessed Englishmen. When their wives and girlfriends had safely gone to bed, Englishmen eagerly tuned in to watch continental mammaries - and happily discussed them with colleagues and friends in the pub and at work. This role has now been allotted to the latest mainstream commercial station, Channel 5. But unlike the intellectually-stimulating Channel Four, the new station appears to have little *raison d'être*, apart from late night titillation with porn so soft it spreads straight from the fridge.

Satellite, cable and digital television have recently become popular in England, particularly on the nation's council estates. This is due, in no small part, to the nation's abhorrence of choice ('What we want is lack of choice, and more of it'). The Sky channels dominating the sector are owned by the international media magnate, Rupert Murdoch. Incidentally, he also owns *The Sun* and *The Times* and enough of the rest of the media to cause genuine concern that he is trying to remake the world in his own image. Some people argue that Mr Murdoch should be applauded for introducing satellite channels into England, but these are people who have never watched them. The diet of soap opera repeats and tedious talk shows is shunned by all but the unemployed, the retired, the mentally incapacitated, students, the entire underclass and most prisoners.

The influence of Murdoch has been felt most keenly in the vital area of soccer. Sky hold the rights to broadcast the country's Premier League games - and its woeful coverage is a national disgrace. The presenters hype the games way beyond the sensibilities of most moderate Englishmen with a relentless and hyperactive barrage of bilge. Aiding them in their commentary are various gadgets and gizmos: the on-screen light pen which is so thick and clumsy it looks like the inside of your screen has been smeared with bird muck, the ridiculous option to follow just one player - as opposed to the whole game - with the 'Sky Player Cam', the annoying 'swooshing' noise that accompanies each action replay. Along with the endless promotion of other Sky products, these elements combine to produce a programme that ought to be banned by the government on the grounds of taste. In the opinion of most right-thinking people, the BBC should be given a monopoly on soccer coverage, the swooshing noise silenced, the light pen snapped and Mr Murdoch jailed for criminal damage to the national game.

The dramatic arts

One of England's most famous sons is William Shakespeare, the sixteenth-century playwright, dramatist and poet. The Bard is considered to be the most cultured Englishman ever and, in the four centuries since his death, no-one has challenged his position. In other words, English culture rests on sixteenth-century laurels. This is unfortunate, as most English people find Shakespeare completely unintelligible.

A deep-seated suspicion of high culture is endemic in English society. While the majority have a passing acquaintance with one of Shakespeare's plays (having been forced to read it at school), they feel his dialogue and subject matter are alien and obsolete. The chattering classes, of course, take extreme issue with this attitude, arguing that Shakespeare's works can speak to a contemporary audience and that his themes have a timeless resonance. They delight in quoting from his plays while criticising the ignorance of the philistine majority. They rarely go and see them, though. This is left to pensioners, parties of reluctant school children, and tourists hoping to get Will's autograph after the show. The foreigner's experience of a Shakespeare play is certainly consistent with the rest of his time in England: he doesn't understand a word anyone says or why they behave so strangely:

Touchstone: Stand you both forth now: stroke your chins and swear by your beards that I am a knave.

Celia: By our beards, if we had them, thou art.

Touchstone: By my knavery, if I had it, then I were; but if you swear by that that is not, you are not forsworn: no more was this knight, swearing by his honour, for he never had any; or, if he had, he had sworn it away before ever he saw those pancakes or that mustard.

...and how the Japanese tour party titters at that little repartee.

The English take great pleasure in their ignorance of the nation's cultural heritage, as the high sales of tabloid newspapers and low audience figures for Shakespeare plays attest. Although it is true that an Englishman asked to name a dramatist will say 'Shakespeare', he is not the only playwright to have written successful dramas. In the contemporary world of television and cinema, English drama has experienced something of a Renaissance. It has achieved this with a series of classy and class-based period dramas such as *The English Patient*, *A Room With A View* and *Shadowlands*. Cunningly, these have been marketed in America as contemporary reportage, and have given the English film industry enormous international cachet (after which, people in England decided they liked them too). They also keep the tourists flooding over to see how life was lived in Edwardian times.

Alas, there has been a welter of lame comedies of late. But, amongst these have been some absolute gems. *Four Weddings and a Funeral* and *Notting Hill* are biting satires on the state of English film-making. In both, Hugh Grant stars as a repressed, stuttering Englishman (symbolising the film industry). And in both, he can only achieve happiness by shagging - sorry, 'having a love affair with' - a plastic, soulless American woman (Andie McDowell and Julia Roberts respectively symbolising Hollywood). The fact that both of these films closely resemble the sort of feeble, arse-licking bilge they were satirising is testament to their genius - and the cause of their success.

Bean caused audiences to almost split their sides (or was it their wrists?) at Rowan Atkinson's magisterial performance as a grotesque, gurgling mute wearing unfashionable clothes and constantly finding himself in ludicrous and humiliating social situations. This damning indictment of England's 'care' of the mentally ill in the community was worthy of Fellini, with a mix of pathos and heart rending humour that has the real potential to change laws and attitudes.

But these commercial successes are by no means the limit of recent English film-making. A nation's cultural reputation is built on a fine balance of commercial and underground, or art-house, successes. In the latter arena, film-makers have counterbalanced the obvious English stereotypes played by the likes of Grant and Atkinson with …obvious English stereotypes played by less well-known actors.

Using this radical new line in self-caricature, *Lock, Stock, and Two Smoking Barrels* cashed in on Sixties gangster chic: cheeky chappy Cockney psychopaths that everybody can love, especially their mothers, and Sixties gangster chicks. Bless. *The Full Monty* chronicled the post-Thatcher decline of traditional industry, revealing the beer belly of modern working-class life, and just a little more besides. Both mercilessly exploited 'types' of Englishman, except they used little-known actors and a smaller budget to do so, and were therefore considered far more original.

There's always some smart Alec ready to sell glib observations on English character to gullible foreigners. This national ironic sense of humour is the direct result of England losing its place as the foremost nation in the world. With the empire disbanded, the factories closed down and the trains running late, the patient English have had to put up with a great deal. But they have found the ideal way to cope with the series of national humiliations: the world laughs at them as they laugh all the way to the bank.

Conclusion

A nation's newspapers, television and dramatic arts are indicative of a nation's cultural health, but the eccentric English patient has a daffodil where the rectal thermometer should be, so it's hard to tell how he's doing. Somewhere between the past and the present lies the truth about the state of English culture, mired between the usual contradictions: a love of bawdiness and a sense of propriety; elitist high culture and entertainment for all. At least everybody can agree that they hate Noel Edmonds and Chris Evans, and so long as this can be stated categorically, there is still a glimmer of hope.

Twelve: AN ENGLISH UNIVERSITY - OXFORD

Superiority breeds contempt

The university town of Oxford provides the ideal vantage-point for our assessment of the English education system, offering further proof of a patient willingness to accept a hierarchy based almost entirely on social class. Thus we find ourselves on a bank of the River Isis in that ancient university city, on an unseasonably mild May afternoon. Muscular rowers glide past as their coxes swear at them in plummy English. Undergraduates amble along, tripping over their long college scarves. Meanwhile academics wearing second-hand anoraks shuffle past creating new theories from the depths of their beards.

Yet the idyllic surroundings cannot help but give rise to a number of vexing questions. Why don't they speak in normal English here? They wear *subfusc* for exams in *literae humaniores*, a scout cleans their room for them, and they call The Thames *The Isis*. What is this pervasive attitude of superiority? Why are the students mummified in their scarves when it's sunny? And how do you pass the dreaded entrance interview?

Visitors to Oxford are taken aback by the architectural splendour of its colleges. Some, like All Souls, defy adequate description with their perfection, although John Keats did attempt it with his 'dreaming spires' poem. Other colleges, such as Christ Church, are dominated by breath-taking quadrangles bigger than most universities. Meanwhile, several colleges are set within extensive acres of land: Magdalen (pronounced 'Maudlin') is one such, boasting an exquisite deer park - and its tutors are noted connoisseurs of the tender venison which regularly appears on the menu at high table. Little wonder, then, that

163

Oxford is viewed with considerable awe by the outside world, and that tourists always outnumber the university's students.

Undergraduates

For much of its history, the job of both ancient universities was to educate those destined, by birth, to run the empire. The essential skills for empire posts were:

- A healthy disdain for the natives.

- An appreciation of literature (there was little else to do but read, drink and screw the natives in the colonial outstations).

- A facility at various sports.

- A well-developed expertise in holding parties for other ex-patriots.

As we might expect, Oxford has changed little over the centuries, despite the disappearance of the empire. The contemporary undergraduate's life is therefore dominated by:

- Constant attempts to humiliate peers in argument and humiliation at the hands of his tutors.

- Endless hours of reading.

- Regular appearances in the college boat or on the college's playing fields.

- A hectic round of cocktail parties, dinner parties and balls.

The chief admissions procedure for Oxford undergraduates is an interview designed to intimidate the prospective student with bizarre questions and psychological games. The typical scene has the interviewer sitting ten yards from the candidate, picking his nose and tossing tangential questions such as, 'Give three reasons for Britney Spears' iconic status among Chinese adolescent girls'. After she has offered a list of socio-economic theories, the interviewer asks why she is wasting her time on pop music instead of studying. There follows a session of sneering at the written work she submitted prior to the interview and repeated demands to justify the subordinate clause in paragraph three of the essay on Romulus and Remus. Most responses are met with a theatrical yawn as the interviewer plots whether to ask the History applicant to draw a 5 dimensional triangle. In short, the sadistic Oxford admissions tutors thoroughly enjoy the interviews. But what about the candidates?

For the aristocrat, subjected to all manner of torture and emotional abuse from an early age, the interview is hardly a cause for concern. This holds true for the upper-middle-class candidate, too. Years of independence from his parents, along with a well-developed superiority complex, allow him to navigate the interviewer's traps with impunity.

The privately-educated offspring of the chattering classes are likewise unfazed, because they occupy the moral high ground of always being right.

It is the less confident middle or working-class genius from a mediocre state school for whom Oxford proves an undiluted hell. His natural reaction to the pervasive arrogance of his university peers and tutors is to leave quickly, commit suicide or quietly study, attain top marks and never return.

Exams

Oxford examinations encourage the undergraduate's sense of superiority and distinction. Candidates are required to wear an outfit known as *subfusc*: a black gown, white shirt, white bow tie, black suit and black shoes. Brightly-coloured socks are strictly banned, while the untying of the bow can lead to immediate suspension. After the undergraduate's final exam, a further convention is strictly followed: the relieved candidate emerges victorious from The Examination Schools and is immediately attacked by a coterie of friends who cover him with a mixture of double cream, milk, flour, Pimms, sparkling white wine and confetti.

Students of other universities take their exams in jeans and Tshirts and, afterwards, they drink alcohol rather than shower in it. No wonder the working class undergraduate feels depressed at Oxford: considerable quantities of money are required to waste whole bottles of Pimms celebrating a friend's final exams, and that's before he's bought the evening's supplies of Bollinger.

Eton's school uniform is remarkably similar to the *subfusc* garb, so public school graduates effortlessly slide into the role of undergraduate, while the working-class scholar feels distinctly ridiculous wearing his borrowed tuxedo as he scribbles down his exam answers. But this is the Oxford way and if the student wants to fit in he must accept its long-cherished traditions. Many Oxford academics argue that they are looking for intellectual potential in their students, as long as free thinking doesn't come with it. So those who supinely accept the blatantly absurd conventions are most suited here.

Sport

Students and tutors alike are proud of their individual colleges: their centuries of academic excellence, their astronomical wealth, their well-stocked wine cellars and their striped scarves. Although intellectual competition is endemic at Oxford, the theme of one-upmanship is most apparent in the sporting arena. Each college vies to make its mark in any number of sports - from rugby and rowing to fives and lacrosse - in the internal university competitions, known as 'Cuppers'.

This emphasis on sporting endeavour provides ideal training for its non-aristocratic students who graduate from Oxford to the City of London. Marathon training sessions, after-event drinking sessions and the obligatory all-night essay-writing sessions gracefully merge into the 20-hour working days and six hour liquid lunches that characterise the rest of their lives in merchant banks and law firms. 'Orandum est ut sit mens sana in corpore sano,' ('You should pray for a healthy mind in a healthy body') the undergraduates repeat, as they slip into their emblazoned sportswear at 5.30 am. The sensible ones, of course, do their praying in bed.

The internal college rivalry is forgotten when the university is faced with competition from Cambridge. This reaches its apogee with the annual varsity matches. The most famous of these is the Boat Race, held each spring on the River Thames in London. The Boat Race attracts millions of viewers and no wonder - they get to see some of the finest student bodies in action. However, the membership of the boats is hardly representative: most university oarsmen are over 25, have rowed for their respective countries and are considerably less intelligent than the undergraduates. The admissions interview for international sportsmen is said to take a predictable course:

Admissions Tutor: Good day. Please take a seat. I see from your application that you rowed at the last Olympics.

Skilled Rower: Yeah, that's about it.

Admissions Tutor: Would you like a scholarship?

Skilled Rower: No, a rowing boat will do.

Admissions Tutor: You misunderstand. A scholarship is a form of remuneration.

Skilled Rower: Well, all right. But I want paying too you know?

Admissions Tutor: Ng! Very well, we'll pay you too (gormless cretin).

This procedure is followed for other sports - rugby union in particular. The rivalry between the two universities at the Varsity match every December means that normally rigorous academic standards are sacrificed so that each player can develop a neck bigger than his brain.

The Rest of the Education System

From the heady vantage point of Oxford, we can appropriately enough look down on the remainder of the English education system. During the Thatcher years, the number of students progressing to higher education grew enormously. Not because the English finally came to value education, but to bleed huge numbers from the unemployment statistics. As a result, English universities now attract those who would have left school at sixteen, thirty years ago (literally in some cases, as mature student numbers are also on the rise). The fact that universities now offer courses in soccer studies and car dealership may illustrate that they are dealing with important contemporary issues and vital sales techniques, or it may simply prove that the government will do anything to reduce the dole queues. In a further twist, students no longer receive grants for tuition fees and living, so the government is actually saving itself money.

As a result of this artificial stuffing of the universities, life therein is very different to that at Oxford. On one of the big, isolated campus universities such as Lancaster, Warwick, or Exeter, the student finds himself in a strange world, populated only by other students. Here, everything is supplied 'on campus' and there is no need to visit the real world. Amidst the concrete union buildings and landscaped landscape, the seeds of political revolution and social change once grew. Now the only things that grow are the multi-storey car parks, to house the increasing numbers of student cars. The days when a student could barely afford a second hand guitar and a tie-dye tablecloth have disappeared, as student loans have taken the place of standing on one's own two feet. Anything is possible with a student loan, but the ethos tends to be: take one out, blow it all on booze or expensive stereo equipment, and have such a good time you fail your degree. You don't have to pay it back until you're earning enough to do so comfortably, so make sure that never happens and absolve yourself of debt. A good system. Okay, England will end up full of third rate second hand car salesmen, but at least they'll have had a good time at Uni.

Higher education follows a hierarchy similar to the social class system. At the top, Oxford and Cambridge are the aristocrats. They are immediately followed by institutions which hanker after the prestige of the ancient universities, but which will never quite have the breeding - several colleges in London, Durham and York fall into this category. Next come the 'red brick' universities in Hull, Leeds, Manchester, Liverpool and Birmingham. And these middle-ranking universities look down on the academic equivalent of the working and underclass - the former polytechnics and colleges of higher education. An educational pyramid where those at the top are treated to the world's best teaching, surrounded by some of England's most beautiful buildings, and those at the bottom struggle to learn in over-crowded concrete carbuncles.

Conclusion

Near the bottom of this pyramid are the teacher training institutes. Trainee teachers are faced with markedly lower entry requirements than, say, vets, who are trained at elite academic institutions. From this we can safely conclude that the English value the health of their pets above the education of their children.

Thirteen: POLITICS

Asleep at the wheels of power

Unlike other countries, England does not have a written constitution to detail the rights of the citizen and the extent of the state's power. Perhaps this is because the English are not citizens, but subjects of the crown. The upper echelons of English society have historically always been far too busy acquiring other people's possessions to bother writing down the rules. As a result, the piecemeal accumulation of customs and conventions means that present-day politics are indecipherable to the vast majority of the patient English. Politicians are therefore treated with a liberal mix of incomprehension, despair and apathy. The English do take a keen interest in political affairs each March, when the chancellor reveals how much extra tax they will pay on their alcohol, cigarettes and petrol. At all other times, they leave it to the chattering classes to discuss politics, while the politicians try to get their names in the papers.

Most of the English, then, do not bother to work out the labyrinthine conventions of their politics. Let's see why.

Structure

English politics are based on the theory of the separation of powers, which is usually held as vital for a democracy to work properly. The theory goes that the three branches of government - executive, legislature and judiciary - ought to be entirely separate, ensuring that citizens' rights are not abused.

In practice, the Queen is head of the executive, ratifies legislation and appoints judges. The Prime Minister and his cabinet colleagues make the executive decisions and are also members of the elected House of Commons or the unelected

House of Lords (the legislature). Meanwhile, the Lord Chancellor manages the judiciary, presides over the House of Lords and is a senior member of the Cabinet, with his unelected fingers in all three pies. The current Lord Chancellor was appointed as a thank-you by Tony Blair for giving him his first job after he had trained as a lawyer. Confused? So are the English. Simply put, English politics do not live up either to democratic ideals, or the theory of the separation of powers. They do, however, live up to the English ideals of hierarchy, hypocrisy and obsessive fidelity to tradition.

In Practice

We begin our analysis in the House of Commons debating chamber, the focus of political debate in England. This is where the Prime Minister and the leader of the opposition engage in their weekly battle of wits at Prime Minister's questions (PMQ). Discussion in the Commons is based on adversarial debating techniques and put-down strategies, so it comes as little surprise that both the PM and the opposition leader are Oxford graduates. Childish point-scoring, amusing one-liners and rhetorical tricks are the bread and butter of the successful English politician. He might also try name calling, jeering and raspberry blowing. PMQ provides one of the few times we find a Full House. The rest of the time you're lucky to get a pair of jokers. During PMQ, the government benches are packed with eager MPs willing to ask the most sycophantic questions in the hope that the PM will give them a government job. The opposition benches are replete with members keen to try their hand at humiliating the PM, in the hope that they will appear on the TV news, or in the broadsheet parliamentary sketch.

Currently, the Conservative (right-wing) party is in opposition. Their leader is a bald, yet schoolboy-ish little twerp called William Hague, who speaks in a strange hybrid of Queen's

English and Yorkshire dialect. The opposition leader gets to ask three questions before some of the backbenchers are allowed a turn, unless he rolls six twice in succession, in which case he gets an extra question or twenty pounds off the banker. Hague often asks difficult questions and is sometimes faintly amusing, though whether MPs are laughing at his jests or his plainly ludicrous manner of speech is uncertain. The PM then answers the questions, having been briefed by his civil servants - whose job it is to guess what the questions will be and then look up the answers in books. But if he gets one wrong, the next round is no conferring. Generally, the PM can relax once he has fended off the leader of the opposition's questions. The MPs on his own side then ask their questions: is his new baby sleeping through, for instance. Meanwhile the opposition members ask stupid questions which the clever civil servants have seen a mile off. The entire house drowns in the noise of what seems to be a seal cull.

For the remainder of the time, the House of Commons is a dull and dreary place, and drowns only in the noise of waffle and snoring.

As we have mentioned, English MPs have no power. They are told how to vote by their leaders. If they disobey commands, there is no chance of their joining the lucrative gravy train of ministerial life and they face the appalling prospect of deselection from their seat - and the necessity of looking for a proper job. It's a hard life: only by making other MPs and journalists laugh can members expect to make a mark. Few MPs are wits. Most are barely half that, and so the vast majority fail. Instead they find themselves lampooned by the wags in the House of Commons press gallery.

There are two types of parliamentary correspondent: those who write lengthy, heavyweight stories about policies, with repercussions posited and statistics listed; and proper journalists. The skilled and amusing writers craft the parliamentary sketch, which takes the 'human angle' on politics, and points to the multitude of MPs' foibles and strange mannerisms. One of the best sketch-writers of the last decade, Matthew Parris of *The Times*, for instance, has focused on the political ramifications of Tony Blair's advancing bald patch. Other sketch-writers have followed his lead, and the discussion of wigs in the Commons is more rife than at any point since the Nineteenth Century. This concentration on politicians' (lack of) hair is explained by the sketch-writers' vantage-point: situated directly above the chamber.

This human angle approach is successful because of the readers' ignorance of politics and also their familiarity with baldness, madness and obesity - three conditions for which members are famed. The human angle is also a reaction to the conventions of parliamentary debate, which are so stultefying even members rarely turn up. Other than PMQ, only occasions of great importance, like the resignation speech of a scandalous minister, or the annual debate on MPs' salaries, attract a majority of members.

The lives of MPs are not only hindered by the dullness of debate and their own intellectual shortcomings: they must also follow an intricate form of address when they speak. A member cannot direct his comments to the person he is addressing, but must use the indirect medium of 'The Speaker'. The Speaker, sitting on an ornately carved, raised seat at the end of the chamber, and wearing a uniform of black garters and cloak, plays the role of the poor child in a loveless marriage:

"Tell your father I'll cut up one of his silk ties every day he's late home."

"Tell your mother to please do so, as she bought me most of them."

This puts the Speaker in an uncomfortable position: shouting

"Order, order" is the only way to calm the crowd. The most famous Speaker in recent years, a former dancer from Yorkshire, used to shout in a gravelly voice whenever her charges become boisterous and unruly, which was most effective for the Conservatives, transporting them back to a childhood under Nanny's skirts.

When an MP refers to a member of his own party, convention dictates that he addresses him as: 'My Honourable Friend, the member for Upper Petheringhole'. Should the MP address a member of a different party, he must not describe him as friend, merely: 'The Honourable Member for Lower Petheringhole', with as much sarcasm as he can muster.

If an MP holds, or has held, an important government position, he is known as a 'Privy Councillor', and is afforded the even more sarcastic title, 'Right Honourable'. The Privy Council used to look after Henry VIII's chamber pot, and included such dignified officers of state as 'The Keeper of the Royal Stool'. With such impressive historical credentials, it is the dream of all politicians to be referred to as 'The Right Honourable'.

If the member is a skilled practitioner of the law, he may already have been given the title 'Queen's council' or 'QC', by the legal authorities. In parliament he must be addressed as 'Learned'.

If an MP should hold all of these positions, members of his party are forced to address him as 'My Right Honourable and Learned Friend, the Member for Lower Petheringhole'.

Politics attracts those of a vain bent, as a rule, and these conventions simply fan the flames of their conceit. Naturally, these rules hardly endear them to the public, simply confirming the suspicion that politicians are ridiculous buffoons who enjoy talking in a funny language. Let us examine if there is any truth to these commonly-held assumptions.

Malpractice?

The life of the average MP is difficult to pin down. Some continue working during their parliamentary careers, finding ample opportunity to practise law, write articles or work as 'political consultants' for shady businesses. Those less prone to the activity of work play computer games, conduct affairs with ambitious, attractive research assistants and drink cheap beer in the many Commons' bars.

Officially, MPs are the representatives of their constituents, required to voice the fears of the people, assisting them in their struggle for justice and democracy. But the patient English rarely contact their elected representative, accepting instead the inevitable farce of the governmental machinery. The only groups who regularly write to their MP are animal lovers, the insane and the chattering classes. For the most part, the MP is able to transfer responsibility for this assortment of troublesome constituents to his assistants. His £40,000-plus office allowance pays both for the latest computer games technology and these handy trouble-shooters.

The professional life of the MP is undemanding and provides real potential for advancement to high governmental office. Promotion is particularly smooth today, as those with talent or intelligence go where the true power lies: The City, the media and the higher reaches of the Civil Service. We shall return to the Civil Service towards the end of the chapter.

The sex life and the dodgy dealings can be demanding, though. One former Cabinet minister, the Right Dishonourable Jonathan Aitken, was sent to prison for lying in court about a couple of free nights he spent in the Paris Ritz when he was a Defence Minister. Other Conservative MPs were caught with brown paper bags full of money which the owner of Harrods, Mohammed Al-Fayed, had given them to ask questions in the House. One of these, Neil Hamilton, took the shop owner to court for libel - and lost. Many other members have been caught with their pants down. Stories of MPs dressing their mistresses in football strips before having sex, MPs having sex with their young researchers when they should have been voting and MPs engaging in dangerous auto-erotic sexual rituals have become an integral feature of political life. As a result of these scandals, MPs who were previously considered boring, pedantic arseholes by the sceptical English voters are now seen as hypocritical, perverted arseholes - a more accurate assessment.

The Lords

The second house of parliament is The Lords, which historically consisted of a bunch of old farts who knew nothing about anything, but claimed to speak for the silent majority. If only this had made them silent farts, they might not have been so contemptible. However, the wind of change has blown through the House of Lords. It now consists of a dwindling number of aristocrats and an increasing number of the Prime Minister's friends. In 1997, the Labour Party promised to remove hereditary peers from The Lords but, like most of their promises, they only partially delivered. The House now comprises 89 hereditary peers, 26 bishops, two royal office holders and almost 600 others appointed by the power of patronage. This interim arrangement will continue while various experts attempt to work out what the Lords actually does. (A difficult task when its responsibilities are not written down anywhere - the generally accepted 'sticking their nose in where it's not wanted' seems a bit vague). The Lords will therefore continue with its hybrid membership: hereditary peers with inherited titles, and life peers, whose positions were given to them by a friendly Prime Minister. This power of patronage on the part of the Prime Minister is not to be dismissed. The present PM, apparently a believer in the democratic principle, has given peerages to his former boss and his former flat-mate, amongst others.

The Noble Lords and Ladies (to give their official titles) debate the issues of the day and hold the government accountable for its actions. By sheer accident of birth or friendship with the Prime Minister (which amounts to the same thing), The Lords takes a full and active role in England's democratic politics.

The seats in the debating chamber of the House of Lords are upholstered in a rather appealing dark red leather, against which it is hard to spot some of the ruddy old darlings. Noble Lords and Ladies sleep soundly through the afternoon's debates, waking sporadically if they suffer a minor stroke or heart palpitation. The majority of the Lords are elderly and infirm. As a result, most suffer from blindness, deafness, Alzheimers Disease, irritable bowel syndrome or arthritis, and many have The Lords disease: trenchfoot of the head, the result of keeping it buried firmly in the sand. The House of Lords is therefore best described as a retirement club for aristocrats and the well-connected, providing companionship, warmth and cheap food during their increasingly incapacitated winter years.

The Lords comes into its own at the annual State Opening of Parliament, when the Queen makes a special guest appearance to read a message from her government. By convention the Lords and Ladies dress up in their traditional regalia of red velvet gowns and ermine collars. It is generally believed they have a splendid time, performing geriatric and arthritic impressions of Zorro, Batman and Wonderwoman. Whether they detract from or contribute to political life is rather a side-issue as virtually no-one reports what they say in their soporific debates.

Head of State

The Nineteenth Century constitutional historian, Bagehot, described the monarch as 'dignified'. By this he did not mean that Queen Victoria was able to take insults without blowing raspberries, but that she was essentially powerless. This is held to be true for the present Queen, but she actually enjoys far more influence than the MPs or Lords. For example, all legislation requires her approval. As the legal consultant for this book succinctly put it, "Without the Queen's royal assent, the law would not be particularly legal". All of which suggests the Queen couldn't be less 'dignified' if she dropped her bloomers and flashed the royal arse.

The Queen is also Head of State, as you'll note if you examine English currency (she's the one with the chins and the neat set of curls). She is also Commander-In-Chief of the armed forces and Supreme Governor of the Church of England. The powers of the

Head of State are said to have diminished over the centuries. When Henry VIII was King of England, few impediments to his absolute power existed. If he took a dislike to one of his subjects, he could simply order the recalcitrant to be 'hung, drawn and quartered', and when the English priests and monks began to annoy him, he stole their land and put them to death.

Now the Queen acts on the advice of her ministers. They in turn act on the advice of their civil servants, who are, in theory, servants of the Crown employed at Her Majesty's pleasure. So where, we might ask, does power lie? We could do worse than to look at Her Majesty's crown servants. But first let us peep at their political masters.

The Prime Minister is generally regarded as the most important person in government. He is the chairman of the Cabinet, where he tells his important colleagues what he has decided to do. He is also the leader of the parliamentary party and, as we have seen, has the power to appoint his friends to the House of Lords. Tony Blair has been a popular Prime Minister, if only because the previous one was so hopeless, and the one before that was inhumane. But his popularity is couched in negative terms - the English view him as 'less bad' than previous incumbents but this is about as good as it gets for a Prime Minister.

Behind the scenes, behind the Prime Minister, English political science is quite simple. The PM, having made promises to the voters at the last election, is keen to change things, but he is faced with a bureaucracy that is quite happy with the way things are, thank you very much. The Oxford-educated mandarin, who has spent his entire professional life in the comfortable confines of Whitehall, is loth to allow anything so transient as an elected politician to disturb things. As a result, he spends his entire professional life soothing the minister's ego, deviously bringing him around to his essentially conservative point of view.

This leads us back to our question of where political power lies. The mandarins control the elected politicians and they owe their positions to the monarch. Happily, mandarins and monarch share the same unerring devotion to the status quo, so HRH lets them get on with it. Political power, then, probably resides somewhere between the top civil servants and the Queen, with the odd minor input from the PM. Everyone else in the political system is mere window dressing. Of course, the patient English accept all this in good faith: what option do they have when no-one's bothered to write down the rules?

Conclusion

The visitor to the Houses of Parliament might reasonably expect to spot politicians going about their daily business but, like the ancient English universities, parliament is a part-time institution. At Christmas, Easter and summer, the Serjeant-at-Arms pokes the slumbering MPs with a stick and orders them to go home for a rest. The summer 'recess' lasts from the middle of July until the end of October.

It is often remarked that members of the teaching profession have it easy with school holidays, but the teacher's holiday entitlement is pitiful compared to the politician's. Unsurprisingly, the patient English do not complain about these scandalously extended leaves of absence - they're just relieved to have a bit of peace, even if it appears that no-one is at the wheels of power.

Fourteen: ENGLAND AND THE OUTSIDE WORLD

From colonisation to confusion

England's relationship with the outside world has followed a familiar pattern of resistance to change and hostility to outsiders. This could be a result of the many invasions England suffered during her early history or a hangover from the violent colonialism with which she wreaked her revenge on the rest of the world. With eyes turned to the past, contemporary England has watched her role as a world power disappear.

America is now the world's major player - a violent country forged by violent Europeans. A gentler breed of European is creating a 'United States of Europe', though England refuses to take part properly, like a sulky child at a party. But before we investigate the position of the patient English on the world stage, let us look closer to home. The English are still viewed as successful imperialists by the Scots, the Welsh and the Northern Irish Catholics, as the overwhelmingly dominant partner in both Great Britain and the United Kingdom.

GB

Great Britain is an amalgam of England, Scotland and Wales - the result of England's historical tendency to invade and colonise at will. Nowadays, the attitude of the Scots and Welsh towards the English has distilled to one of loathing, jealousy and apathy.

Since the Act of Union in 1707, the Scots have felt a deep resentment towards the English *sassenach*. This anti-English sentiment manifests itself most obviously when England play sport, an English defeat leading to untold celebration north of the border. When Scotland beat England, the entire country comes to a Scotch-induced standstill.

The Scots have an ingrained pride in their country and they cherish their symbols of nationhood: the thistle, the flag of St Andrew, the national anthem (*Flower of Scotland*) and, of course, their kilts. This highly-developed sense of national identity is a direct reaction to defeat and colonisation at the hands of the English.

In recent times, nationalist arguments for outright independence from Great Britain have gained popularity. With the suave former Bond actor, Sean Connery, on their side, nationalists are currently riding high in the opinion polls. Connery loves his country so much, he'd rather live abroad than pay English taxes. In 1998, Scotland was granted its own parliament with limited powers separate to the British Parliament at Westminster. Many Scots see this as but the first step towards a break-up of the union with England.

Meanwhile, the Welsh sense of nationhood, while less intense than that of the Scots, is clearly discernible, especially in the north of the country. Wales was colonised well before Scotland, resulting in a greater degree of assimilation, particularly in the English-speaking south. Welsh opinion of the English is therefore split, with outright antipathy in the north and total apathy in the south. In north Wales they hang on to their language, their *Eisteddfords* and their hostility to the English who own holiday homes there. In 1998, a slightly more ambiguous Welsh assembly was granted limited powers to sit on the floor and sing *All Things Bright and Beautiful*.

UK

The United Kingdom is Great Britain with the addition of Northern Ireland. Anglo-Irish relations have been far from smooth: Northern Ireland has been a battle zone for the last 30 years, with frequent skirmishes on the British mainland. Nationalist and unionist communities have been unable to live together without constant tit-for-tat killings: the 'you killed one of ours, so we'll kill one of yours' mentality is like a truce with bullets. Recent developments have, however, allowed an uneasy peace to develop, and Northern Ireland has been granted its own assembly. But Catholics in Northern Ireland still feel an intense sense of injustice at what they consider to be an arrogant occupying power. Meanwhile, the Protestant Northern Irish make a considerable show of their loyalty to the British state, crown and flag which is equally baffling to the reticent English.

Visitors

Britain and the United Kingdom are hardly a cause of controversy for the English. They see their Celtic and Northern Irish neighbours as eccentrically hot-tempered over institutions established a long time ago. The English view both Great Britain and the United Kingdom as mere historical accidents, and fail to see what all the fuss is about - perhaps because it was them doing the invading. Let us see.

The last time England was invaded was the Norman conquest of 1066. Whatever sense of national identity England had then was already shaped by the Romans, Vikings and Saxons who'd been before (though the horned bowler hat never really caught on). Since then, England has welcomed immigrants from all over the globe, but expected them to accept the nation's abiding cultural mores.

When the Irish arrived during the 19th century, they congregated in particular areas of cities and were treated with suspicion by their host population. Today's fourth and fifth generation immigrants have just about been acclimatised into the patient English mainstream. The same goes for Polish, Italian and Jewish immigrants.

Newcomers from the Indian sub-Continent and the West Indies forty-odd years ago now find their third and fourth generations gradually being anglicised, though no-one will pretend this has been easy. Racism still has a worrying resonance. The English do not like change and are suspicious of anything new. But immigration from the Commonwealth has forced the English to look more deeply at themselves and realise that most of them are immigrants themselves - they just don't sound like foreigners anymore.

Nationhood

English history is packed with incidents of bloodthirsty, arrogant behaviour. It is no longer considered politically correct, for example, to enter a sovereign territory, butcher its inhabitants and then impose one's own laws and language on the native populace. The English used to be good at this, but now imperialism is a dirty word, and human rights are finally considered important. Celebrating the success of colonialism and the blatant abuse of basic human rights would look a little churlish now. In any case, given that football hooligans and racists have hijacked patriotism, the English feel slightly queasy about being over-enthusiastic about their country. When the well-behaved majority of English football fans see the monosyllabic lout laying in with fist and boot just because their team lost, they wonder whether this patriotism lark is really worth the trouble.

The English have therefore become rather blasé about the business of patriotism, certainly in comparison to their neighbours. They are proud of England, and Britain, and the United Kingdom, but for the English these institutions seemed synonymous - all, in essence, the same. So devolution has come like the breaking of a spell. Now these little nations, formerly part of the family can speak for themselves. It's limited speech as yet, but instead of bawling unnoticed, they can now say, "Mummy, you're a bitch".

Europe is trickier. England is physically part of Europe, but only because of the Channel Tunnel. It feels an acute sense of isolation. If the tunnel were an ear trumpet, the English could lift it and hear the rest of Europe complaining about being ruled by Brussels too. Unfortunately, the belief of standing alone against the world is a typically English trait.

And what about the outside world? England has had close ties with many other countries: the shadow of its Empire still falls across the Commonwealth, spanning vast tracts of Africa, North America, Asia and Oceania. And though the Commonwealth is little more than a talking shop, it is a reminder that the English are not a historically inward-looking nation.

On the flip-side, the English are suspicious of foreigners; they do not learn foreign languages, because everyone else learns English, they are irritated by tourist's in their own country, but when they go on holiday - to Spain or Greece - they make sure the resorts are full of English chippies, English tabloids and English lager.

CONCLUSION

Confusion.

Conclusion

Fifteen: THE END?

English patience rewarded

We have arrived at the end of our journey through the pitfalls and frustrations in the lives of the patient English. But the English themselves are a long way from finishing their own long journey. They have won - and lost - more than most other countries could dream of. An empire for one thing. The World Cup for another. And the small matter of world economic domination. The English have watched these historical developments with a patient sigh and a wistful sense of having seen it all before. But as they enter their third millennium, is it fair to write off the English? In short, have the patient English had it?

The English are richer, they live longer and have a more balanced diet than at any time in their history (the rise of the curry being responsible for this last fact). More of the English than ever before own their own homes and gardens - with the resultant boom in trade for DIY stores and garden centres. English unemployment has been virtually eradicated, with the result that peak period commuter traffic jams are longer than ever before. Indeed, the government's coffers are so full that the Chancellor of the Exchequer appears faintly embarrassed on Budget Day when he raises taxes on cigarettes, alcohol and fuel. "I'm only doing this for your own good - I really don't need the cash," he thinks to himself, safe in the knowledge that the patient English will pay up.

The English have not experienced revolution or defeat in war - at least during recent centuries. As a result, change has been incremental and slow. The Germans and Japanese had to start from scratch after the Second World War. The Americans and French have revolutionary traditions. The English, meanwhile, have simply carried on and made do with what they already have.

Of course, England has its problems. Excessive drinking leads to scenes of violent disorder every weekend. The obsession with social class means snobbery is rife. And it rains too much. But England's pubs give the English upper lip a necessary degree of flexibility. The class hierarchy allows the Royal Family to attract tourists. And the almost constant cloud cover means England's rate of skin cancer is low in the international context.

The patient English are, then, far from finished. They now take full advantage of their two main assets: their language and their past. Financial services and tourism have replaced textiles and mining, as the English come to terms with a new world order. Clinching multi-million dollar deals in plush offices and dressing up as Henry VIII at Hampton Court are more fun and less dirty than standing in front of a sewing machine or hewing coal, so the English are happier in their work.

In short, the patient English are not standing still. No - they just appear to be when you see them stuck in the queue at the post office, or sitting in a 20-mile jam on the M1.